Lessons Learned on Compliance and Ethics

The Best from the FCPA Compliance and Ethics Blog

Thomas Fox

Ethics 360 Media

Lessons Learned on Compliance and Ethics:
The Best from the FCPA Compliance and Ethics Blog

By Thomas Fox

Ethics 360 Media

Information in this book is intended for public discussion and educational purposes only. It does not constitute legal advice and its use does not create an attorney-client relationship.

ISBN 978-981-07-1347-8

Acknowledgements

There are three people who were instrumental in inspiring me, suggesting to and getting me through the slog of writing this book. Francine McKenna helped start me on my journey in compliance and her advice that '*if you want to work in compliance, keep your eye on the ball*' is something I think about quite often. Dick Cassin has been a mentor and a guiding light in the arena of compliance and it was he who suggested I write this book. And finally to my wife, Michele Rudland who has tirelessly supported me in this journey into the field of compliance, who has stood by me and buoyed and buttressed me the entire time AND, most importantly, is the Editor of this book. Thanks to all of you and the best of my love to Michele.

Foreword by Richard L. Cassin

Tom Fox's outstanding FCPA Compliance and Ethics Blog is daily reading for corporate counsel and compliance officers around the world. Every one of his many fans (myself included) knows that when Tom talks about compliance, we should listen.

Although he's a Texan, Tom is no 'cowboy' when it comes to compliance. He's thoughtful, deliberate, and conscientious. That's why his views about the Foreign Corrupt Practice Act, the UK Bribery Act, and similar laws have real weight. And why his blog posts, some of the best of which are collected in this book, are widely recognized as essential reading for anyone in the compliance community.

What sets Tom and his work apart? For one thing, he's generous. His authoritative posts are accessible to everyone free of charge. And he shares himself with his readers too.

He once explained in a post why you often see 'box scores' on his blog – from FCPA-related prison sentences, to how long it takes companies to disclose compliance problems, and many more. He said,

> I am an avid baseball fan and as a child, was taught how to keep score at professional baseball games by my Grandfather. This had two effects. The first was immediate; it kept

> me quiet at ballgames. The second is more long term; I continue to keep score at baseball games up to the present.

And Tom keeps readers up to date by sharing the latest compliance trends. It was from one of his posts (included in this book) that I learned what 'provenance' means in the context of supply-chain compliance. 'Transparency instead of opaqueness' he explained, 'a new focus on quality, safety, ethics and environmental impact' – all good news.

But there's a lot more to Tom than a string of industry-changing blog posts, however momentous that body of work is. There's his unflinching focus on compliance. About every enforcement action, Tom asks: 'What does this teach about how to comply with the anti-corruption laws?'

That's Tom's constant target, his Holy Grail. Always. In that sense, Tom is true to his Texas roots – solid, committed, and unwavering. Great traits for anyone who spends his days helping people and the companies they work for comply with the FCPA and laws like it. That helps explain why Tom has so many devoted readers, fans, and friends.

Whether you've known his work for a while or are new to it, I'm sure you'll enjoy every page of this fine book as much as I did. It shows Tom Fox at his best – and in the compliance world, it doesn't get any better than that.

Preface by
J. Daniel Chapman

My earliest memory of Tom Fox is from a legal conference about ten years ago where we both were delivering speeches. Following a lengthy and detailed presentation by a lawyer from a prestigious law firm, Tom leaned forward to his microphone and said, "Well, from the perspective of an in-house counsel, here is what you really need to know..." In a matter of seconds, he then proceeded to explain several of the complex concepts covered by the previous speaker in simple, concise and understandable language.

In the years since that conference, Tom and I worked together on variety of projects as co-presenters at other conferences, on benchmarking efforts and as attorney and client. Throughout this time, he always maintained the same approach to sharing information and providing legal advice. His approach has been and remains to succinctly convey his message in terms easily grasped by his audience.

Tom originally refined his ability to communicate complicated legal requirements into practical advice during his many years of service as an in-house legal counsel, including his appointment as the general counsel for a company facing significant compliance issues related to the U.S. Foreign Corrupt Practices Act. In these positions Tom implemented a variety of compliance solutions, internal controls, policies and training programs designed to address bribery risks. In addition to this in-house experience, Tom also has the advantage and perspective acquired from conducting multiple anti-bribery investigations while in private practice. This book captures the benefits of all of Tom's experience and, in doing so, will be valuable to any legal practitioner dealing with anti-bribery and corruption issues.

The content of this book is generally derived from Tom's industry-recognized FCPA Compliance and Ethics blog. While the blog format is well-suited to Tom's style because of its free-flowing and colloquial nature, its use can be helpful to any legal counsel advising companies about anti-bribery compliance. In particular, the blog format is written in a manner that is recognizable to a business person, and it reminds us of how we should communicate with our clients in the modern world.

These two influences, Tom's experience and the blog format, have helped shape this book into a superior tool for attorneys. This book is an effective, reliable resource for lawyers, and it provides the precedents and examples that lawyers need to save time for themselves and their clients. The chapter on the "nuts-and-bolts" of a compliance program displays these benefits well; it outlines the key elements of an effective anti-bribery compliance program without digressing into other topics solely for the sake of demonstrating the comprehensiveness of the work product. This straightforward approach presents the efficiency that is needed by many lawyers either who do not focus their practice on anti-bribery compliance or who have other substantial responsibilities. Furthermore, it is especially useful to in-house counsel, who often are forced by time limitations to choose between addressing immediate problems and establishing the compliance programs that would have prevented them.

This book is a reflection of Tom Fox at his best. In

each of its chapters, he takes a position supported by the strongest legal arguments and simply tells us what needs to be done to achieve compliance. There is no doubt that many lawyers will come to rely upon this book as a key resource for explaining the essential elements of anti-bribery compliance to their clients.

Lessons Learned on Compliance and Ethics

The Best from the FCPA Compliance and Ethics Blog

Contents

CHAPTER I

SOME THOUGHT ON BEST PRACTICES

An Effective FCPA Compliance Program - by Lanny Breuer

Posted June 2, 2010

At the recent Compliance Week 2010 Annual Conference one of the issues discussed by Assistant Attorney General, for the Criminal Division of the US Department of Justice, Lanny Breuer, was what the Department of Justice (DOJ) might consider as an "effective compliance and ethics program" under the Foreign Corrupt Practices Act (FCPA), if a FCPA violation occurs and a company's compliance program comes under scrutiny from the Criminal Division of the DOJ. We believe that Breuer gave the conference attendees quite a bit of information that can be utilized by companies in crafting and evaluating their compliance policies.

Breuer noted that the most effective type of compliance program is one that "prevents fraud and corruption in the first place but when such compliance program has not done so, there are defined policies in place to "quickly detect, fix and report the [FCPA] violations." Additionally, an effective compliance program should not be static but dynamic to meet changing business circumstances, such as when a company might move to doing business in a high risk country. Effective compliance programs should also be ever-evolving through continued assessments, as the compliance world grows and matures. Breuer cited two source material references as benchmarks; he listed

(1) the Principles of Federal Prosecution of Business Organization and its full section on corporate compliance programs and (2) the OECD Good Practice Guidance on Internal Controls, Ethics, and Compliance.

Breuer then delineated several elements that the Criminal Division would evaluate in assessing a company's compliance program, should a FCPA violation occur.

- Does your company have an effective compliance "Tone at the Top"; so that the Board and CEO are demonstrated to be fully committed to an effective compliance program?
- A company's compliance program should not only punish compliance violations, through termination, other disciplinary actions or reduction in or denial of bonus but should also reward good ethical behavior in a corporation by promotion of ethical employees or other rewards such as a significant component of an overall bonus program. Regarding employee discipline, Breuer emphasized the DOJ would review all circumstances surrounding a company's decision regarding discipline but that any "superficial steps" would not impress the DOJ.
- A company should have a strong whistle-blower program through a hotline or other appropriate mechanism and protection for any employee who reports such conduct through anonymous reporting and a clear no-retaliation policy.
- The compliance function led by a person with senior level management authority, the overall compliance function should have clear reporting lines to such senior level employee and such person should have a direct reporting by a company's compliance officer to the company's Board of Directors.
- There should be periodic reviews of a company's

compliance program, utilizing internal resources such as a company's Internal Audit function and outside professional consultants.

- A company's effective compliance program should be extended directly into foreign business partners, such as agents, distributors, reseller and joint venture partners.

Breuer ended this portion of his talk by re-emphasizing that the DOJ was not only interested in your company's compliance program but also other companies with whom you might be doing business with and the effectiveness (or lack thereof) of their compliance program. This would not only extend to foreign business partners but also those companies in your Supply Chain and conceivably down to your customer base.

So do you have an "effective compliance program" as outlined by Lanny Breuer?

FCPA Settlement Day: DOJ Guidance on the Best Practices of a Corporate Compliance Program

Posted November 4, 2010

In what the FCPA Blog termed a day of making history "for the most companies to simultaneously settle FCPA-related violations, [the] Global logistics firm Panalpina and five of its oil-and-gas services customers resolved charges with the DOJ and SEC, and another customer settled with the SEC only", the Department of Justice (DOJ) and Securities and Exchange Commission (SEC) announced settlements which totaled fines, penalties and profit disgorgements of over $236.5 million. The FCPA Professor noted that while the "DOJ and SEC enforcement actions principally focused on customs and related payments in Nigeria, but also including alleged improper conduct in Angola, Brazil, Russia, Kazakhstan, Venezuela, India, Mexico, Saudi Arabia, the Republic of Congo, Libya, Azerbaijan, Turkmenistan, Gabon and Equatorial Guinea." He also noted that since July, "the U.S. government has brought FCPA enforcement actions totaling approximately $1.1 billion" in fines, penalties and profit disgorgement.

However, more was announced yesterday than simply raw dollars. Each resolved enforcement action provided to the Foreign Corrupt Practices Act (FCPA) compliance practitioner significant information on the most current

DOJ thinking on what constitutes a *best practice* FCPA program. Each of the Deferred Prosecution Agreements (DPA) released yesterday, included an Attachment C, a document entitled "Corporate Compliance Program". Each Corporate Compliance Program was the same in all the DPAs announced yesterday. Each Corporate Compliance Program detailed the latest *best practices* its internal controls, policies, and procedures regarding compliance with the FCPA. (This same information was also attached to the Noble Non-Prosecution Agreement (NPA) as "Attachment B".)

The information included these collective Corporate Compliance Programs provides the FCPA compliance practitioner with the most current components that the DOJ believes should be included in a FCPA compliance program. Hence, this information is a valuable tool by which companies can assess if they need to adopt new, or to modify their existing, internal controls, policies and procedures in order to ensure that their FCPA compliance program maintains: (a) a system of internal accounting controls designed to ensure that a Company makes and keeps fair and accurate books, records and accounts; and (b) a rigorous anti-corruption compliance code, standards and procedures designed to detect and deter violations of the FCPA and other applicable anti-corruption laws.

The Preamble to each Corporate Compliance Program noted that these suggestions are the "minimum" which should be a part of a Company's existing internal controls, policies and procedures. Each Corporate Compliance Program had thirteen points which are set out below. They are:

1. Code of Conduct. A Company should develop and promulgate a clearly articulated and visible corporate policy against violations of the FCPA, including its anti-bribery, books and records, and internal controls provisions, and other applicable foreign law counterparts (collectively, the "anti-corruption laws"), which policy should be memorialized in a written compliance code.

2. Tone at the Top. The Company will ensure that its senior management provides strong, explicit, and visible support and commitment to its corporate policy against violations of the anti-corruption laws and its compliance code.

3. Anti-Corruption Policies and Procedures. A Company should develop and promulgate compliance standards and procedures designed to reduce the prospect of violations of the anti-corruption laws and the Company's compliance code, and the Company should take appropriate measures to encourage and support the observance of ethics and compliance standards and procedures against foreign bribery by personnel at all levels of the company. These anti-corruption standards and procedures shall apply to all directors, officers, and employees and, where necessary and appropriate, outside parties acting on behalf of the Company in a foreign jurisdiction, including but not limited to, agents and intermediaries, consultants, representatives, distributors, teaming partners, contractors and suppliers, consortia, and joint venture partners (collectively, "agents and business partners"), to the extent that agents and business partners may be employed under the Company's corporate policy. The Company shall notify all employees that compliance with the standards and procedures is the duty of individuals at all levels of the company. Such standards and procedures shall include policies governing:

a. gifts;
b. hospitality, entertainment, and expenses;
c. customer travel;
d. political contributions;
e. charitable donations and sponsorships;

f. facilitation payments; and

g. solicitation and extortion.

4. Use of Risk Assessment. A Company should develop these compliance standards and procedures, including internal controls, ethics, and compliance programs on the basis of a risk assessment addressing the individual circumstances of the Company, in particular the foreign bribery risks facing the Company, including, but not limited to, its geographical organization, interactions with various types and levels of government officials, industrial sectors of operation, involvement in joint venture arrangements, importance of licenses and permits in the company's operations, degree of governmental oversight and inspection, and volume and importance of goods and personnel clearing through customs and immigration.

5. Annual Review. A Company should review its anti-corruption compliance standards and procedures, including internal controls, ethics, and compliance programs, no less than annually, and update them as appropriate, taking into account relevant developments in the field and evolving international and industry standards, and update and adapt them as necessary to ensure their continued effectiveness.

6. Sr. Management Oversight and Reporting. A Company should assign responsibility to one or more senior corporate executives of the Company for the implementation and oversight of the Company's anti-corruption policies, standards, and procedures. Such corporate official(s) shall have direct reporting obligations to the Company's Legal Counsel or Legal Director as well as the Company's independent monitoring bodies, including internal audit, the Board of Directors, or any appropriate committee of the Board of Directors, and shall have an adequate level of autonomy from management as well as sufficient resources and authority to maintain such autonomy.

7. Internal Controls. A Company should ensure that it has a system of financial and accounting procedures, including a system of internal controls, reasonably designed to ensure the maintenance of fair and accurate books, records, and accounts to ensure that they cannot be used for the purpose of foreign bribery or concealing such bribery.

8. Training. A Company should implement mechanisms designed to ensure that its anti-corruption policies, standards, and procedures are communicated effectively to all directors, officers, employees, and, where necessary and appropriate, agents and business partners. These mechanisms shall include: (a) periodic training for all directors and officers, and, where necessary and appropriate, employees, agents, and business partners; and (b) annual certifications by all such directors and officers, and, where necessary and appropriate, employees, agents, and business partners, certifying compliance with the training requirements.

9. Ongoing Advice and Guidance. The Company should establish or maintain an effective system for:

a. Providing guidance and advice to directors, officers, employees, and, where necessary and appropriate, agents and business partners, on complying with the Company's anti-corruption compliance policies, standards, and procedures, including when they need advice on an urgent basis or in any foreign jurisdiction in which the Company operates;

b. Internal and, where possible, confidential reporting by, and protection of, directors, officers, employees, and, where necessary and appropriate, agents and business partners, not willing to violate professional standards or ethics under instructions or pressure from hierarchical superiors, as well as for directors, officers, employees, and, where appropriate, agents and business partners, willing to report breaches of the law or professional standards or ethics concerning anticorruption occurring within the company, suspected criminal conduct, and/or violations of the compliance policies, standards, and procedures regarding the anticorruption laws for directors, officers, employees, and, where necessary and appropriate, agents and business partners; and

c. Responding to such requests and undertaking necessary and appropriate action in response to such reports.

10. Discipline. A Company should have appropriate disciplinary procedures to address, among other things, violations of the anti-corruption laws and the Company's anti-corruption compliance code, policies, and procedures by the Company's directors, officers, and employees. A Company should implement procedures to ensure that where misconduct is discovered, reasonable steps are taken to remedy the harm resulting from such misconduct, and to ensure that appropriate steps are taken to prevent further similar misconduct, including assessing the internal controls, ethics, and compliance program and making modifications necessary to ensure the program is effective.

11. Use of Agents and Other Business Partners. To the extent that the use of agents and business partners is permitted at all by the Company, it should institute appropriate due diligence and compliance requirements pertaining to the retention and oversight of all agents and business partners, including:

a. Properly documented risk-based due diligence pertaining to the hiring and appropriate and regular oversight of agents and business partners;

b. Informing agents and business partners of the Company's commitment to abiding by laws on the prohibitions against foreign bribery, and of the Company's ethics and compliance standards and procedures and other measures for preventing and detecting such bribery; and

c. Seeking a reciprocal commitment from agents and business partners.

12. Contractual Compliance Terms and Conditions. A Company should include standard provisions in agreements, contracts, and renewals thereof with all agents and business partners that are reasonably calculated to prevent violations of the anticorruption laws, which may, depending upon the circumstances, include: (a) anticorruption representations and undertakings relating to compliance with the anticorruption laws; (b) rights to conduct audits of the books and records of the agent or business partner to ensure compliance with the foregoing; and (c) rights to terminate an agent or business partner as a result of any breach of anti-corruption laws, and regulations or representations and undertakings related to such matters.

13. Ongoing Assessment. A Company should conduct periodic review and testing of its anticorruption compliance code, standards, and procedures designed to evaluate and improve their effectiveness in preventing and detecting violations of anticorruption laws and the Company's anti-corruption code, standards and procedures, taking into account relevant developments in the field and evolving international and industry standards.

What are the Elements of an Effective FCPA Compliance Program? Berland on the OECD Good Practice Guidance on Internal Controls, Ethics, and Compliance

Posted June 4, 2010

In our last blog posting we discussed the speech by Assistant Attorney General, for the Criminal Division of the US Department of Justice (DOJ), Lanny Breuer at the Compliance Week 2010 Annual Conference where he outlined what he believed are elements of an effective FCPA compliance program. One of the sources Breuer cited as a benchmark is the Organization for Economic Co-operation and Development (OECD) Good Practice Guidance on Internal Controls, Ethics, and Compliance. We were therefore pleased when we received a copy of this quarter's Society of Corporate Compliance and Ethics Magazine (SCCE) (Vol. 7 / No. 3) and found an article by our colleague Russ Berland on this source material referenced by Breuer in his talk.

Berland began with a background discussion of the genesis of the Working Group on Bribery in International Transactions Organization for the OECD and its development of the specific elements of a compliance program. In his article Berland, lists 12 specific instructions for companies to utilize as a basis to construct an effective compliance program upon. They are:

1. A culture of compliance with the appropriate "tone at the top".
2. Clearly articulated and visible policy against bribery and corruption.
3. It must be the duty of every employee to company with a company's anti-bribery program.
4. One or more senior officers in charge of the compliance program who must report directly to the Board or appropriate Board Committee.
5. Design the compliance program to prevent and detect bribery and corruption.
6. Make the program applicable to third party business partners.
7. Have a system of internal financial controls in place to ensure that bribery and corruption cannot be hidden.
8. Have periodic communications and training on the compliance program.
9. Provide positive support for employees to comply with the compliance program.
10. Consistently discipline employees for violations of the compliance program.
11. Provide guidance and advice for employees on the compliance program.
12. The compliance program should be periodically re-assessed and re-evaluated to take into account new developments.

Near the end of his article, Berland asks the question, will DOJ prosecutors find a company's FCPA compliance program "effectively designed when it was based on the OECD guidance?" Much like Socrates (in that he knows the answer to his question), Berland responds "The answer should be yes." We heartily agree and thank Russ for his much needed article providing specific guidance on what the OECD finds to be the elements of an effective compliance program.

Changes Coming: US Sentencing Guidelines, UK Bribery Bill and the OECD on Facilitation Payments - Part I

Posted April 14, 2010

At its April 7, 2010 meeting the United States Sentencing Commission (USSC) approved amendments to its Sentencing Guidelines. The next day on April 8, 2010, the UK Bribery Bill received Royal Assent. These two events follow the December 9, 2009 release by the Organization for Economic Co-Operation and Development's (OECD) *Recommendation for Further Combating Bribery of Foreign Public Officials*, when the OECD marked the tenth anniversary of the entry into force of the OECD Anti-Bribery Convention.

These three releases, which comprise of two changes in the legal schemes by two of the world's largest economic players and the proposal of one of the largest Non-Governmental Organizations (NGO) dedicated to ending corruption across the globe, portend significant changes in how companies will be structured and transact business going forward in the new decade. This will be the first of three postings in which we will discuss the changes that companies, with any US or UK presence, will be required to implement. The initial post will be on the changes to the US *Sentencing Guidelines*; in our second post, we will then consider the changes required by the UK *Bribery Bill*; and in our third and final post, we will end with the recommendation as found in the OECD's *Recommendation for Further Combating Bribery of Foreign Public Officials* regarding the ending of facilitation payments.

The US Sentencing Guidelines are used in the sentencing of organizations and serve as the de facto blueprint for corporate ethics and compliance programs. The changes, which were approved at the April meeting, must be formally submitted to Congress by May 1, and will take effect November 1, 2010, unless Congress passes legislation to reject or modify them. These proposed changes follow public hearings and public comment period which ended in March. The most significant changes in the Sentencing Guidelines are as follows.

1. Direct Report. The amendment would change the reporting structure in corporations where the Chief Compliance Officer (CCO) reports to the General Counsel (GC) rather than a committee on the Board of Directors. The proposed change reads "the individual... with operational responsibility for the compliance and ethics program...have direct reporting obligations to the governing authority or any appropriate subgroup... (e.g. an audit committee or the board of directors)". If a company has the CCO reporting to the GC, who then reports to the Board, such structure may not qualify as an effective compliance and ethics program under the Sentencing Guidelines. The better practice would now appear to be that the CCO should be a direct report to the Board or appropriate subcommittee of the Board such as compliance or audit.

2. Discovery of Problem Inside the Organization Rather Than Outside. This amendment encourages a company to have a hotline and other mechanisms to detect any compliance and ethics violations internally. While most companies have a Code of Conduct, with attendant implementation policies and procedures in place, training thereon and a hotline; many companies have yet to implement any type of self-audit program to measure Foreign Corrupt Practices Act (FCPA) compliance program performance. This encourages companies to not only monitor its internal self-reporting to actively test the information available to it through a system such as continuous controls monitoring.

3. Promptly Report. This amendment inserts specific language regarding the "prompt" reporting of any violation of a compliance and ethics program. While no definition of the word "prompt" is provided, the revisions to the Commentary note that an organization will be "allowed a reasonable time to conduct and internal investigation" and that no reporting is required if "... the organization reasonably concluded...that no offense has been committed". Nevertheless, this language reiterates what many former Department of Justice (DOJ) employees tell industry representative at conferences and events regarding the FCPA. It is *always* preferable to report a violation to the US government rather than the US government finding out and coming to you.

4. No Person With Operational Responsibility Condoned or Was Willfully Ignorant. This proposed amendment is aimed at those personnel within a company's compliance and ethics organization. While operational responsibility could be defined to mean only those who might report to the Board, this commentator would suggest the better approach is to include all company personnel with direct reporting responsibility in the compliance and ethics group. The definition of "willfully ignorant" has not changed from the current version of the Sentencing Guidelines, which is provided in Application Note 3 of Commentary to §8A1.2 (Application Instructions-Organizations). The definition reads in full "An individual was "willfully ignorant of the offense" if the individual did not investigate the possible occurrence of unlawful conduct despite knowledge of circumstances that would lead a reasonable person to investigate whether unlawful conduct had occurred".

Changes Coming: US Sentencing Guidelines, UK Bribery Bill and the OECD on Facilitation Payments - Part II

Posted April 16, 2010

At its April 7, 2010 meeting the United States Sentencing Commission (USSC) approved amendments to its Sentencing Guidelines. The next day on April 8, 2010, the UK Bribery Bill received Royal Assent. These two events follow the December 9, 2009 release by the Organization for Economic Co-Operation and Development's (OECD) *Recommendation for Further Combating Bribery of Foreign Public Officials*, when the OECD marked the tenth anniversary of the entry into force of the OECD Anti-Bribery Convention.

These three releases, which comprise of two changes in the legal schemes by two of the world's largest economic players and the proposal of one of the largest Non-Governmental Organizations (NGO) dedicated to ending corruption across the globe portend significant changes in how companies will be structured and transact business going forward in the new decade. To follow on from our initial post, this is the second of three postings in which we discuss the changes that companies, with any US or UK presence, will be required to implement. In the initial post we discussed the changes to the US *Sentencing Guidelines*; this post will consider the changes required by the UK *Bribery Bill;* and in the third and final post we will consider the recommendations as found in the OECD's *Recommendation for Further Combating Bribery of Foreign Public Officials* regarding ending of facilitation payments.

There are several differences between the US Foreign Corrupt Practices Act (FPCA) and the UK Bribery Bill which all companies should understand. These include:

- The Bribery Bill
    - ◊ Has no exception for facilitation payments.
    - ◊ Creates strict liability of corporate offense for the failure of a corporate official to prevent bribery.
    - ◊ Specifically prohibits the bribery or attempted bribery of private citizens, not just governmental officials.
    - ◊ Not only bans the actual or attempted bribery of private citizens and public officials but all the receipt of such bribes.
    - ◊ Has criminal penalties of up to 10 years per offense not 5 years as under the FCPA.

There is one affirmative defense listed in the Bribery Bill and it is listed as the "adequate procedures" defense. The Explanatory Notes to the Bribery Bill indicate that this narrow defense would allow a corporation to put forward credible evidence that it had adequate procedures in place to prevent persons associated from committing bribery offences. The legislation requires the Secretary of State for Justice to publish guidance on procedures that relevant commercial organizations can put in place to prevent bribery by persons associated with their entity.

Other than this commentary, the Bill provides no further information on what might constitute "adequate procedures" as a defense; however, the Government has signaled that it will work with the UK business community to provide appropriate guidance to this critical component of the Bribery Bill. The UK law firm KattenMuchin has indicated that they expect the Government will apply a test regarding the "adequate procedures" defense "with regard to the size of the company, its business sector and the degree to which it operates in high risk markets". The law firm of Covington and Burling, in a client advisory dated March 31, 2010, has opined that the Bribery Bill will not come into force until late 2010 because it will take the UK government until then to issue guidance on what may constitute "adequate procedures".

The Bribery Bill is a significant departure for the UK in the area of foreign anti-corruption. It cannot be emphasized too strongly that the Bribery Bill is significantly stronger than the FCPA. The Bribery Bill provides for two general types of offence: bribing and being bribed, and for two further specific offences of bribing a foreign public official and corporate failure to prevent bribery. All the offences apply to behavior taking place either inside the UK, or outside it provided the person has a "close connection" with the UK. A person has a "close connection" if they were, at the relevant time, among other things, a British citizen, an individual ordinarily resident in the UK, or a body incorporated under the law of any part of the UK. Many internationally focused US companies have offices in the UK or employ UK citizens in their world-wide operations. This legislation could open them to prosecution in the UK under a law similar to, but stronger than, the relevant US legislation.

These changes include the outright banning of facilitation payments and the outright banning of all bribery and corrupt payments by US companies to not only foreign governmental officials but all private citizens. The Bribery Bill certainly does away with any legal question of "who is a foreign governmental official". The FCPA, and through the use of other legislation such as the Travel Act, bans bribery generally, to back corrupt actions made to a foreign person who is not a governmental official, into an FCPA violation. All US companies with UK subsidiaries or UK citizens as employees, should ban such acts as part of their overall compliance and ethics policies sooner rather than later.

Changes Coming: US Sentencing Guidelines, UK Bribery Bill and the OECD on Facilitation Payments - Part III

Posted April 21, 2010

At its April 7, 2010 meeting the United States Sentencing Commission approved amendments to its Sentencing Guidelines. The next day on April 8, 2010, the UK Bribery Bill received Royal Assent. These two events follow the December 9, 2009 release by the Organization for Economic Co-Operation and Development's (OECD) *Recommendation for Further Combating Bribery of Foreign Public Officials*, when the OECD marked the tenth anniversary of the entry into force of the OECD Anti-Bribery Convention.

These three releases, which comprise of two changes in the legal schemes by two of the world's largest economic players and the proposal of one of the largest Non-Governmental Organizations (NGO) dedicated to ending corruption across the globe portend significant changes in how companies will be structured and transact business going forward in the new decade. This is the third and final of three postings which have discussed the changes that companies, with any US or UK presence, will be required to implement. In the initial post we considered the changes to the US *Sentencing Guidelines*; we then discussed the changes required by the UK *Bribery Bill*; and in this final post, we will end with the recommendations regarding facilitation payments as found in the OECD's *Recommendation for Further Combating Bribery of Foreign Public Officials*.

The OECD and Facilitation Payments

In late 2009, to celebrate "International Anti-Corruption Day" recognizing the Tenth Anniversary of the OECD Anti-Bribery Convention, the OECD released "The Recommendation for Further Combating Bribery of Foreign Public Officials". In this report the OECD recommended changes relating to facilitation payments (aka "grease payments") such as those which are legal under the US Foreign Corrupt Practices Act (FCPA). OECD Secretary-General Angel Gurría described these low-level payments, designed to expedite performance of a "routine government action" such as obtaining mail delivery, phone or power service, as "corrosive . . . particularly on sustainable economic development and the rule of law".

Facilitation payments, also known as "expediting payments" or "grease payments," are bribes paid to induce foreign officials to perform routine functions they are otherwise obligated to perform. Examples of such routine functions include issuing licenses or permits and installing telephone lines and other basic services. The only countries that permit facilitation payments are the United States, Canada, Australia, New Zealand and South Korea. Facilitation payments, however, are illegal in every country in which they are paid. They have come under increasing fire under the FCPA as inconsistent with the totality of US policy on anticorruption.

This change by the OECD brings the considerable problems associated with facilitation in the international business arena into sharper focus. Just like large commercial bribes, grease payments abuse the public trust and corrode corporate governance. Treating them as anything other than outright bribery muddies the compliance waters and adds confusion where there should be clarity. This new stance by the OECD, coupled with the increased enforcement under the FCPA, may well bode the end of facilitation payments. There is no monetary threshold for determining when a payment crosses the line between a facilitation payment and a bribe. The accounting provisions of the FCPA require that facilitation payments must be accurately reflected in an issuer's books and records, even if the payment itself is permissible under the anti-bribery provisions of the law.

Facilitation payments carry legal risks even if they are permitted under the anti-bribery laws of a particular country. In the US enforcement agencies have taken a narrow view of the exception and have successfully prosecuted FCPA violations stemming from payments that could arguably be considered permissible facilitation payments. Violations of the accounting and recordkeeping provisions of the FCPA are also more likely when a company makes facilitation payments. Abroad, countries are increasingly enforcing domestic bribery laws that prohibit such payments. Companies that allow facilitation payments face a slippery slope to educate their employees on the nuances of permissible payments in order to avoid prosecution for prohibited bribes.

The global business environment has changed even as the FCPA has remained static. In the absence of any legislative action to roll back the facilitation payment exception, the US Department of Justice (DOJ) and Securities and Exchange Commission (SEC) plainly have set out to repeal the facilitation payment exception on a case-by-case basis. US companies should recognize the weakening of the argument supporting a facilitation payment exception and should develop compliance policies that do not permit any kind of grease payments. A policy that prohibits all payments (unless there is high level of legal and compliance approval) will relieve businesses of the compliance burden of differentiating between lawful and unlawful payments. From the point of view of the modern global corporation, a compliance regime that attempts to differentiate between "good" corrupt payments and "bad" corrupt payments will do more harm than good.

US Sentencing Guidelines Changes Become Effective November 1

Posted November 2, 2010

Yesterday, on November 1, 2010, the proposed changes in the US *Sentencing Guidelines* became effective. This post will highlight the changes and what they may import for the Foreign Corrupt Practices Act (FCPA) compliance professional. The US Sentencing Guidelines are used in the sentencing of organizations and serve as the de facto blueprint for corporate ethics and compliance programs. The changes, which were approved at an April meeting of the US Sentencing Commission and were formally submitted to Congress by May 1, became effective yesterday. These proposed changes followed public hearings and public comment period which ended in March. The most significant changes in the Sentencing Guidelines are as follows.

1. Direct Report. The amendment changed the reporting structure in corporations where the Chief Compliance Officer (CCO) reports to the General Counsel (GC) rather than a committee on the Board of Directors. The change reads "the individual...with operational responsibility for the compliance and ethics program... have direct reporting obligations to the governing authority or any appropriate subgroup... (e.g. an audit committee or the board of directors)". If a company has the CCO reporting to the GC, who then reports to the Board, such structure may not qualify as an effective compliance and ethics program under the amended Sentencing Guidelines. The better practice would now appear to be that the CCO should be a direct report to the Board or appropriate subcommittee of the Board such as compliance or audit.

2. Discovery of Problem Inside the Organization Rather Than Outside. This amendment encourages a company to have a hotline and other mechanisms to detect any compliance and ethics violations internally. While most companies have a Code of Conduct, with attendant implementation policies and procedures in place, training thereon and a hotline; many companies have yet to implement any type of self-audit program to measure FCPA compliance program performance. This encourages companies to not only monitor its internal self-reporting to actively test the information available to it through a system such as continuous controls monitoring.

3. Promptly Report. This amendment inserts specific language regarding the "prompt" reporting of any violation of a compliance and ethics program. While no definition of the word "prompt" is provided, the revisions to the Commentary note that an organization will be "allowed a reasonable time to conduct and internal investigation" and that no reporting is required if "... the organization reasonably concluded...that no offense has been committed". Nevertheless, this language reiterates what many former Department of Justice (DOJ) employees tell industry representative at conferences and events regarding the FCPA. It is *always* preferable to report a violation to the US government rather than the US government finding out and coming to you.

4. No Person With Operational Responsibility Condoned or Was Willfully Ignorant. This proposed amendment is aimed at those personnel within a company's compliance and ethics organization. While operational responsibility could be defined to mean only those who might report to the Board, this commentator would suggest the better approach is to include all company personnel with direct reporting responsibility in the compliance and ethics group. The definition of "willfully ignorant" has not changed from the current version of the Sentencing Guidelines, which is provided in Application Note 3 of Commentary to §8A1.2 (Application Instructions-Organizations). The definition reads in full "An individual was "willfully ignorant of the offense" if the individual did not investigate the possible occurrence of unlawful conduct despite knowledge of circumstances that would lead a reasonable person to investigate whether unlawful conduct had occurred".

All companies subject to the FCPA should review their compliance policies and procedures to ascertain if they are in compliance with these changes. With the up and coming effective date of the UK Bribery Act on April 1, 2011, companies should have a comprehensive review of their compliance program to determine if any changes need to be made.

The End of the FCPA Facilitation Payment Exception?

Posted November 12, 2010

In November, 2009 the Organization for Economic Co-operation and Development (OECD) announced a new recommendation at the OECD's celebration of "International Anti-Corruption Day" and the Tenth Anniversary of the "Entry into Force of the OECD Anti-Bribery Convention". This change relates to facilitation payments (aka "grease payments") which remain legal under the Foreign Corrupt Practices Act (FCPA).

OECD Secretary-General Angel Gurría described these low-level payments, designed to expedite performance of a "routine government action", such as obtaining mail delivery, phone or power service, as "corrosive . . . particularly on sustainable economic development and the rule of law".

Facilitation payments, also known as "expediting payments" or "grease payments" are bribes paid to induce foreign officials to perform routine functions they are otherwise obligated to perform. Examples of such routine functions include issuing licenses or permits and installing telephone lines and other basic services. The only countries that permit facilitation payments are the United States, Canada, Australia, New Zealand and South Korea. Facilitation payments, however, are illegal in every country in which they are paid. They have come under increasing fire under the FCPA as inconsistent with the totality of US policy on anticorruption.

This change by the OECD brings the considerable problems associated with facilitation in the international business arena into keener focus. Just like large commercial bribes, grease payments abuse the public trust and corrode corporate governance. Treating them as anything other than outright bribery muddies the compliance waters and adds confusion where there should be clarity. This new stance by the OECD, coupled with the passage of the UK Bribery Act which bans facilitation payments and increased enforcement under the FCPA, may well bode the end of facilitation payments.

I. TRACE Facilitation Payments Benchmark Survey

In October, 2009, TRACE International published the results of its "Facilitation Payments Benchmark Survey". TRACE conducted a global survey with the following objectives: (1) to understand how facilitation payments are perceived in the international business community, including the level of risk they are deemed to pose and the compliance challenges they present; and (2) to map corporate policies on facilitation payments, including whether they are permitted and, if so, the types of safeguards corporations impose on their payment.

The results of the TRACE survey reveal a definitive move by corporations to ban facilitation payments, coupled with an awareness of the added risk and complexity presented by facilitation payments:

- 76% of survey respondents believe it is possible to do business successfully without making facilitation payments given sufficient management support and careful planning.
- Over 70% believe that employees of their company either never, or only rarely, make facilitation payments, even if their corporate policy permits

facilitation payments.

- Over 93% revealed that their job would be easier, or at least no different, if facilitation payments were prohibited in every country.
- Nearly 44% reported that their corporations prohibit facilitation payments or simply do not address them because facilitation payments are prohibited together with other forms of bribery.
- Almost 60% of respondents reported that facilitation payments pose a medium to high risk of books and records violations or violations of other internal controls.
- Over 50% believe a company is moderately to highly likely to face a government investigation or prosecution related to facilitation payments in the country in which the company is headquartered.

II. Facilitation Payments under the FCPA

The original version of the FCPA, enacted in 1977, contained an exception for payments made to non-US officials who performed duties that were "essentially ministerial or clerical". In 1988 Congress responded by amending the FCPA under the *Omnibus Trade and Competitiveness Act* to clarify the scope of the FCPA's prohibitions on bribery, including the scope of permitted facilitation payments. An expanded definition of "routine governmental action" was included in the final version of the bill, reflecting the intent of Congress that the exceptions apply only to the performance of duties listed in the subcategories of the statute and actions of a similar nature. Congress also meant to make clear that "ordinarily and commonly performed actions", with respect to permits or licenses, would not include those governmental approvals involving an exercise of discretion by a government official where the actions are the functional equivalent of "obtaining or retaining business for, or with, or directing business to, any person".

The FCPA now contains an explicit exception to the bribery prohibition for any "facilitation or expediting payment to a foreign official, political party, or party official for the purpose of which is to expedite or to secure the performance of a routine governmental action by a foreign official, political party, or party official". "Routine government action" does not include any decision by a public official to award new business or continue existing business with a particular party. The statute lists examples of what is considered a "routine governmental action" including:

- obtaining permits, licenses, or other official documents to qualify a person to do business in a country;
- processing government papers, such as visas or work orders;
- providing police protection, mail pick-up and delivery, or scheduling inspections associated with contract performance or transit of goods across country;
- providing phone service, power and water supply, loading and unloading cargo, or protecting perishable products from deterioration; and
- actions of a similar nature

There is no monetary threshold for determining when a payment crosses the line between a facilitation payment and a bribe. The accounting provisions of the FCPA require that facilitation payments must be accurately reflected in an issuer's books and records, even if the payment itself is permissible under the anti-bribery provisions of the law

III. Risks associated with relying on the "facilitation payments" exception

Facilitation payments carry legal risks even if they are permitted under the anti-bribery laws of a particular country. In the US, enforcement agencies have taken a narrow view of the exception and have successfully prosecuted FCPA violations stemming from payments that could arguably be considered permissible facilitation payments. Violations of the accounting and recordkeeping provisions of the FCPA are also more likely when a company makes facilitation payments. Abroad, countries are increasingly enforcing domestic bribery laws that prohibit such payments. Companies that allow facilitation payments face a slippery slope to educate their employees on the nuances of permissible payments in order to avoid prosecution for prohibited bribes.

A. US enforcement authorities construe the exception narrowly

Other than as discussed above, there is no definitive guidance on circumstances in which the facilitation payments exception applies. There may be less risk of enforcement by US authorities in cases involving bona fide facilitation payments that are made specifically for one of the purposes enumerated in the FCPA. However, companies still face the risk of at least facing a governmental inquiry to explain the circumstances surrounding the payments, possibly resulting in penalties based on an unanticipated restrictive interpretation of the exception. As noted by the FCPA Professor, the recent Noble Non-Prosecution Agreement (NPA) noted that the payments made by Noble's Nigerian customs' agent Panalpina, to facilitate the importation of its rigs into Nigeria, did "not constitute facilitation payments for routine governmental actions within the meaning of the FCPA"

B. Potential non-compliance with the FCPA's accounting and recordkeeping provisions

While the anti-bribery provisions of the FCPA permit facilitation payments, the accounting and recordkeeping provisions of the law nevertheless requires companies making such payments to accurately record them in their books and records. Companies or individuals may be reluctant to properly record such payments, as it shows some semblance of impropriety and effectively creates a permanent record of a violation of local law. However, failure to properly record such expenditures may result in prosecution by the Securities and Exchange Commission (SEC) even if the underlying payments themselves are permissible. One example of prosecution resulting from the misreporting of seemingly permissible facilitation payments involves Triton Energy Corporation, which settled an investigation by the SEC involving multiple alleged FCPA violations, including the miss-recording of facilitation payments. An Indonesian subsidiary of the company had been making monthly payments, of approximately $1,000, to low-level employees of a state-owned oil company, in order to assure the timely processing of monthly crude oil revenues. The SEC did not charge that these payments violated the anti-bribery provisions of the FCPA; however, these payments were miss-recorded in corporate books and therefore violated the FCPA's accounting and recordkeeping provisions. Triton Energy consented to an injunction against future violations of the FCPA and was fined $300,000.

C. Increased enforcement of non-US laws that do not recognize an exception for facilitation payments

While the FCPA and certain other national anti-bribery laws contain exceptions for facilitation payments, such payments typically are considered illegal in the country in which they are made; there is not any country in which facilitation payments to public officials of that country are permitted under the written law of the recipient's country. Accordingly, even if a particular facilitation payment qualifies for an exception of the FCPA, it, nevertheless, is likely to constitute a violation of local law – as well as under anti-bribery laws of other countries that also might apply simultaneously – and thus exposes the payer, his employer and/or related parties to prosecution in one or more jurisdictions. While enforcement to date in this area has been limited increased global attention to corruption makes future action more likely. Countries that are eager to be seen as combating corruption are prosecuting the payment of small bribes with greater frequency.

D. Corporate approaches to facilitation payments may exceed the legitimate scope and applicability of the exception

As demonstrated in the TRACE Benchmark Survey, businesses struggle with how to address the "facilitation payments" exception in their compliance policy and procedures, if the subject is covered at all. Businesses should be wary of allowing employees to decide on their own whether a particular payment is permissible. Unless such payments are barred completely or each payment is subject to pre-approval (which in many cases would be unrealistic (e.g., passport control)), there is always the risk that an employee, agent or other person whose actions may be attributed to the company will make a payment in reliance on the exception when in fact the exception does not apply. In addition, the temptation to improperly record otherwise permissible facilitation payments has been discussed above.

IV. End of facilitation payments?

The global business environment has changed even as the FCPA has remained static. After his prepared remarks at the Compliance Week 2010 Annual Conference, Assistant Attorney General for the Criminal Division of the US Department of Justice, Lanny Breuer, took several questions from the audience. One of his more interesting responses was regarding facilitation payments and whether the US was moving towards the OECD/UK Bribery Act model of not allowing such payments. He responded that it was a question which needed consideration as compliance standards are evolving on a worldwide basis. However, as of this date, Breuer was not aware of any proposed change in the FCPA on this issue but that it may be visited in the not too distant future.

US companies should recognize the weakening of the argument supporting a facilitation payment exception and should develop compliance policies that do not permit any kind of grease payments. A policy that prohibits all payments (unless there is high level of legal and compliance approval) will relieve businesses of the compliance burden of differentiating between lawful and unlawful payments. From the point of view of the modern global corporation, a compliance regime that attempts to differentiate between "good" corrupt payments and "bad" corrupt payments will do more harm than good.

CHAPTER II

THE NUTS AND BOLTS OF FCPA COMPLIANCE

Risk-Based Compliance

Posted March 1, 2010

A recent benchmarking survey of Third Party Codes of Conduct was conducted by the Society of Corporate Compliance and Ethics (SCCE) and reported on by Rebecca Walker. The findings indicated that a majority of companies with an otherwise robust compliance program do not extend this to third parties with which they conduct business. The findings revealed the following: 53% of companies do not disseminate their internal codes of conduct to third parties; only 26% require third parties to certify to their own codes; and just 17% of the respondents have any third party codes of conduct.

For those companies which now desire to evaluate their third party business partners for Foreign Corrupt Practices Act (FCPA) compliance, how, and perhaps where, do they begin? The approach that appears to be gaining the most traction both with regulators and learned commentators is to develop a risk based approach to FCPA compliance. There is no specific US Department of Justice (DOJ) guidance on any one specific process for a risk based compliance system. However, there is sufficient guidance in other FCPA and analogous compliance areas, such that direction can be provided to US and foreign companies in this area.

Writing in the FCPA Blog, Scott Moritz of Daylight Forensic & Advisory suggested that a risk-based approach built upon the regulatory programs in Anti-Money

Laundering (AML) governance. In the AML areas, the concept is that certain parties, including vendors, represent a higher compliance risk than others. Geography, nexus to government officials, business type, method of payment and dollar volume - are all risk indicators.

This risk-based approach was commented upon, favorably by the DOJ, in Opinion Release 08-02. In this Opinion Release the DOJ reviewed and approved Halliburton's proposed acquisition of the UK entity Expro. The DOJ spoke directly to a risk based approach by that Halliburton had agreed to provide the following:

> . . . a comprehensive, risk-based FCPA and anti-corruption due diligence work plan which will address, among other things, the use of agents and other third parties; commercial dealings with state-owned customers; any joint venture, teaming or consortium arrangements; customs and immigration matters; tax matters; and any government licenses and permits. Such work plan will organize the due diligence effort into high risk, medium risk, and lowest risk elements.

This risk-based approach has also been accepted by UK's Financial Services Authority (FSA) in its settlement of the enforcement action against the insurance giant AON earlier this year. As a part of the settlement AON agreed to the following:

> AON...designed and implemented a global anti-corruption policy ... limiting the use of third parties ... whose only service to AON is assisting it in the obtaining and retaining of business solely through client introductions in countries where the risk of corrupt practices is anything other than low. These jurisdictions are defined by reference to an internationally

> accepted corruption perceptions index. Any use of third parties not prohibited by the policy must be reviewed and approved in accordance with global anti-corruption protocols.

How does a company implement this guidance? Scott Moritz suggests that key to any risk-based approach is "the strategic use of information technology, tracking and sorting the critical elements -- including risk-ranking, as well as enhanced due diligence and ongoing monitoring of high-risk parties proportionate to their risk profiles."

The uses of a risk based compliance system can be myriad. The Opinion Release 08-02 system was in response to an international acquisition. Such systems can also be used to rank and assist in the evaluation of business partners or supply chain vendors. But, however such a system is used, the clear import from the DOJ, FSA and learned commentators is that some type of rational system should be put in place and followed.

Ongoing Compliance Assessments: FCPA, UK Bribery Act and OCED Best Practices

Posted October 16, 2010

One of the requirements consistent throughout the Principles of Federal Prosecution of Business Organization (US Sentencing Guidelines) and its section on corporate compliance programs; the Organization for Economic Co-operation and Development (OECD) Good Practice Guidance on Internal Controls, Ethics, and Compliance, and the UK Bribery Act's Consultative Guidance is the need for continued assessment of an anti-corruption and anti-bribery compliance program. This posting will review the specifics of each of these documents and will provide to the compliance and ethics practitioner some ideas on how to implement what each of these protocols stress are key components of any *best practices* compliance program.

US Sentencing Guidelines

The US Sentencing Guidelines state that there should be periodic reviews of a company's compliance program, utilizing internal resources, such as a company's Internal Audit function, and outside professional consultants. The OECD Good Practice states that a compliance program should be periodically re-assessed and re-evaluated to take into account any new developments. The UK Bribery Act Consultative Guidance, recently released by the UK Ministry of Justice, requires ongoing monitoring and review by noting that a compliance program and procedures should be reviewed regularly and a company should consider whether an "external verification [of the compliance program] would help."

Speaking at the Compliance Week 2010 Annual Conference, Assistant Attorney General for the Criminal Division of the US Department of Justice, Lanny Breuer, indicated that such an external verification or assurance of the effectiveness of a compliance program is a key component to assist a company in maintaining a 'best practices' Foreign Corrupt Practices Act (FCPA) compliance program. He noted that it is through a mechanism such as an ongoing assessment that a company could continue to evaluate its own compliance program with reference to compliance standards which are evolving on a worldwide basis.

OECD

In this same speech, Breuer cited as a benchmark for a *best practices* compliance and ethics program the protocols set forth in the OECD Good Practice Guidance on Internal Controls, Ethics, and Compliance. In this protocol the OECD suggested that "periodic reviews of the ethics and compliance programs or measures, designed to evaluate and improve their effectiveness in preventing and detecting foreign bribery, taking into account relevant developments in the field, and evolving international and industry standards." Writing in the Society of Corporate Compliance and Ethics Magazine (SCCE) (Vol. 7 / No. 3), Russ Berland explained that this guidance meant that companies should regularly reassess their anti-bribery and anti-corruption compliance program to evaluate and improve its overall effectiveness. Although he did not give a time frame for this regular assessment, Berland noted that any such assessment "should take into account new developments in the area and evolving standards.

UK Bribery Act

Principle Six of the UK Bribery Act's Consultation Guidance discusses the need for ongoing monitoring and review. The Principle states "*The commercial organisation institutes monitoring and review mechanisms to ensure compliance with relevant policies and procedures and identifies any issues as they arise. The organisation implements improvements where appropriate*." The reasons for this continued monitoring was to ensure that if external events, like government changes, corruption convictions, or negative press reports occur, an appropriate compliance response is triggered. The Guidance noted that it would be prudent for companies to consult the publications of relevant trade bodies or regulators that could highlight examples of good or bad practice. Organizations should also ensure that their procedures take account of external methods of issue identification and reporting as a result of the statutory requirements applying to their supporting institutions, for example money laundering regulations reporting by accountants and solicitors.

The Consultative Guidance provided advice for companies which covered several specific suggestions. The senior management of higher risk and larger organizations may wish to consider whether to commission external verification or assurance of the effectiveness of anti-bribery and anti-corruption policies. An independent review can provide to a company, which is undergoing structural change or entering new markets, with an insight into the strengths and weaknesses of its anti-bribery policies and procedures and in identifying areas for improvement. Such independent assessment would also enhance a company's credibility with business partners or help to restore market confidence following the discovery of a bribery incident, to help meet the requirements of both voluntary or industry initiatives and any future pre-qualification requirements.

Ongoing Assessment as 'Best Practices'

All three cornerstones of guidance available to the FCPA compliance practitioner include ongoing assessments as a key component of any *best practices* program. The text of each document and the remarks by commentators make clear the reasons for such an ongoing assessment. Not only do *best practices* evolve but companies and businesses evolve. An assessment is key to measuring where your program currently stands to allow you to know where it needs to be updated.

Attention should be paid to who and how the assessment is conducted. The entity, be it a law firm; professional consultant or other, which designed the FCPA compliance program for your company should not be the assessor. Such assessment would obviously be a conflict of interest. Additionally, a drafter usually has blind spots when assessing one's own work. An outside FCPA compliance professional should be engaged to assess your compliance policy, at no less than every two years, to review and make recommendations to keep your program at the *best practices* standard.

A Hotline as a FCPA Compliance Tool

Posted August 5, 2010

Employees are a company's best source of information about what is going on in the company. It is certainly a best practice for a company to listen to its own employees, particularly to help improve its processes and procedures. But more than listening to its employees, a company should provide a safe and secure route for employees to escalate their concerns. This is the underlying rationale behind an anonymous reporting system within any organization. This concept is one key component of a Foreign Corrupt Practices Act (FCPA) compliance and ethics 'best practices' program. Both the Principles of Federal Prosecution of Business Organization (US Sentencing Guidelines) and the OECD Good Practice Guidance on Internal Controls, Ethics, and Compliance (OCED Good Practices) list, as one of their components, an anonymous reporting mechanism by which employees can report compliance and ethics violations. This concept, in the FCPA world, is usually referred to as a "Hotline". This article will discuss how the use of a Hotline can assist a company with its overall FCPA compliance and ethics efforts.

The US Sentencing Guidelines state:

> (C) to have and publicize a system, which may include mechanisms that allow for anonymity or confidentiality, whereby the

> organization's employees and agents may report or seek guidance regarding potential or actual criminal conduct without fear of retaliation.

The OECD Good Practices states:

> v) companies to provide channels for communication by, and protection of, persons not willing to violate professional standards or ethics under instructions or pressure from hierarchical superiors, as well as for persons willing to report breaches of the law or professional standards or ethics occurring within the company in good faith and on reasonable grounds, and should encourage companies to take appropriate action based on such reporting;

Confidential reporting is critical to any organization, not only from the legal requirements which specify that such a mechanism be available for employees, but also to allow escalation of compliance and ethics issues in a manner which is safe for employees and can lead the discovery of significant FCPA compliance issues. Two recent examples of employees reporting issues include the Daimler and, the ongoing, Avon matters. A company's commitment to a Hotline provides a means by which employees can elevate compliance and ethics concerns before they become full blown FCPA enforcements actions.

While there is no generally accepted industry standard regarding the implementation and employment of a Hotline, EthicsPoint, in a White Paper entitled "It's Not Your Father's Hotline", suggested the following as the 'best practices' for internal Hotlines:

1. *Availability* - A Hotline should be available 24 hours a day/7 days a week and toll-free. It should be

available in the native tongue of the person utilizing it so if your work force uses more than one language for inter-company communications, your Hotline should reflect this as well.

2. *Escalation* - After a report is received through the Hotline it should be distributed to the appropriate person or department for action and oversight. This would also include resolution of the information presented, if warranted and consistent application of the investigation process throughout the pendency of the matter.
3. *Follow-Up* - There should be a mechanism for follow-up with the Hotline reporter, even if the report is made anonymously. This allows the appropriate person within your organization to substantiate the report or obtain additional information at an early stage, if appropriate.
4. *Oversight* - The information communicated through the Hotline should be available to the appropriate Board Committee or Management Committee in the form of statistical summaries and that an audit trail is available to the appropriate oversight group to ensure actions are taken and resolution of any information is reported through the Hotline.

The Hotline can be a key company tool in an effective FCPA compliance program. Properly advertised and then utilized, it can assist a company to learn about issues and take appropriate actions before these issues erupt into more serious problems. Lastly, the proper maintenance of a Hotline can not only allow a company to track compliance issues as they come into the system and document its response but also use this information as an ongoing audit of its FCPA compliance system.

What is your FCPA Investigation Protocol?

Posted September 17, 2010

Speaking at the IQPC 2010 Internal and Regulatory Investigations in Oil and Gas Conference, Dominic Sheils, Compliance Counsel for John Wood Group PLC, and James W. Noe, Senior Vice President, General Counsel and Compliance Officer for Hercules Offshore Inc., discussed two different approaches to internal investigation protocols and how these different approaches work for their respective companies. The presentations of Sheils and Noe highlighted the different approaches taken by many companies in the United States and abroad when dealing with the issue of whether to have a written procedure outlining the steps to be taken when a claim, which may constitute a bribery or corruption, is reported to the company.

Compliance Counsel Sheils indicated that the John Wood Group has a detailed written procedure for handling any such complaint or allegation of bribery or corruption, regardless of the means through which it is communicated. The mechanism could include the internal company hot-line, anonymous tips, or a report directly from the business unit involved. In the John Wood Group the decision on whether or not to investigate is made by the internal Compliance Department, with possible consultation with the Audit Committee of the Board of Directors. The head of the business unit in which the claim arose is notified that such an allegation has been made and that the Compliance

Department will be handling the matter on a go-forward basis.

The John Wood Group uses this detailed written procedure to ensure there is complete transparency on the rights and obligations of all parties once an allegation is made. This allows the Compliance Department to have not only the flexibility but also the responsibility to deal with such matters. The Compliance Department believes that this mandated responsibility gives it the role in which it can best assess and then make a decision on how to manage the matter.

The previous approach is contrasted by that of Hercules Offshore Inc., General Counsel Noe who stated that Hercules has no written protocol for the handling of investigations of allegations of corruption or bribery. He initially noted that he, as General Counsel, makes the final decision on whether a matter is to be investigated. He believes that it is important for the General Counsel to maintain maximum flexibility to deal with the issues involved around any such allegations.

Mr. Noe stated that each investigation depends on the underlying facts presented. He is concerned that if there is a written protocol mandating the procedure it might impinge on the flexibility of the company to proceed. He used the phrase “Sometimes small streams can become big rivers”, indicating that when a matter is thoroughly investigated flexibility is required. Additionally, at Hercules, there is no set person(s) or personnel who are required to be notified when bribery and corruption allegations are put forward. The scope of the decision on to whom and how to make the notification can be influenced by a myriad of factors including statutorily mandated reporting requirements of US public companies, so no one protocol can respond to every scenario.

Both John Wood Group and Hercules Offshore

Inc., have robust Foreign Corrupt Practices Act (FCPA) compliance and ethics programs. Their respective compliance programs differ on the mechanism by which the decisions on investigation protocols and notification are to be made, after an allegation of bribery and corruption comes forward. However, both have made their approaches work for them.

FCPA Compliance Contract Template

Posted September 29, 2010

Speaking at the Seventh Annual IQPC Advanced Contracts Risks Management for Oil and Gas Conference, Don Butler, General Counsel of Seneca Resources discussed contract templates and the use of these documents in transactional work. The concepts which Mr. Butler discussed are applicable when drafting templates which include language related to Foreign Corrupt Practices Act (FCPA) contractual terms.

He began his presentation by noting that by use of the word 'template' he meant that it was a form of contract drafted by his company for use in certain transactions. It was designed to be more than just a starting point for negotiations. The template has several benefits for Seneca which, as he related, include: (1) the language is tested against real events; (2) the language assists the company in managing its risks; (3) the language fits into a series of related contracts; (4) the language is straight-forward to administer and (5) the language helps to manage the expectations of both contracting parties.

The contracting concepts are equally applicable to contracts which a company, subject to the FCPA or UK Bribery Act, would enter into with a foreign business partner such as an agent, distributor, reseller, joint venture partner or any other person or entity which might represent a US or UK business internationally. Such templates must have compliance obligations stated directly in the document, whether such document is a simple agency or consulting agreement or a joint venture with several formation documents. The FCPA compliance language should include representations that in all undertakings the foreign business partner will make no payments of money, or anything of value, nor will such be offered, promised or paid, directly or indirectly, to any foreign officials, political parties, party officials, candidates for public or political party office, to influence the acts of such officials, political parties, party officials, or candidates in their official capacity, to induce them to use their influence with a government to obtain or retain business or gain an improper advantage in connection with any business venture or contract in which the Company is a participant.

In addition to the above affirmative statements regarding conduct, a FCPA template contract should have the following compliance terms and conditions in a foreign business partner contract.

- Indemnification: Full indemnification for any FCPA violation, including all costs for the underlying investigation.
- Cooperation: Require full cooperation with any ethics and compliance investigation, specifically including the review of foreign business partner emails and bank accounts relating to your Company's use of the foreign business partner.
- Material Breach of Contract: Any FCPA violation is made a material breach of contract, with no notice and opportunity to cure. Further such a finding will be the grounds for immediate cessation of all payments.
- No Sub-Vendors (without approval): The foreign business partner must agree that it will not hire an agent, subcontractor or consultant without the Company's prior written consent (to be based on

adequate due diligence).

- Audit Rights: An additional key element of a contract between a US Company and a foreign business partner should include the retention of audit rights. These audit rights must exceed the simple audit rights associated with the financial relationship between the parties and must allow a full review of all FCPA related compliance procedures such as those for meeting with foreign governmental officials and compliance related training.
- Acknowledgment: The foreign business partner should specifically acknowledge the applicability of the FCPA to the business relationship as well as any country or regional anti-corruption or anti-bribery laws which apply to either the foreign business partner or business relationship.
- On-going Training: Require that the top management of the foreign business partner and all persons performing services on your behalf shall receive FCPA compliance training.
- Annual Certification: Require an annual certification stating that the foreign business partner has not engaged in any conduct that violates the FCPA or any applicable laws, nor is it aware of any such conduct.
- Re-qualification: Require the foreign business partner re-qualify as a business partner at a regular interval of no greater than every three years.

Traditional contracting techniques are a useful tool in the FCPA contracting area. By having such template language, a company can put forward the compliance terms and conditions which will not only communicate the foreign business partner's FCPA compliance obligations but also protect a business, to the highest degree possible, through risk shifting-clauses.

So what is in your FCPA contract template?

Effective Ethics and Compliance Training

Posted January 19, 2010

"Conducting effective training programs" is listed in the 2005 US Federal Sentencing Guidelines as one of the factors the Department of Justice (DOJ) will take into account when a company accused of a Foreign Corrupt Practices Act (FCPA) violation is being evaluated for a sentence reduction. As per the Sentencing Guidelines mandate, "(4) (A) The organization shall take reasonable steps to communicate periodically and in a practical manner its standards and procedures, and other aspects of the compliance and ethics program, to the individuals referred to in subdivision (B) by conducting effective training programs and otherwise disseminating information appropriate to such individuals' respective roles and responsibilities." In addition to the Sentencing Guidelines, compliance professionals have also noted the importance of training to handle ethical and compliance issues which arise. In the results of its 2009 Survey on "Anticipating and Planning for the Next Big Compliance Issue", the Society of Corporate Compliance and Ethics (SCCE) participants responded that effective training was "an essential part of the solution."

I. Approaches

But what is an "effective training program"? Andrea Wrage has written in her blog *Wrageblog* and *Ethisphere Magazine* that she believes there are two general approaches to ethics and compliance training. The first approach focuses on knowledge of the rules "as clear and sharp as barbed wire" so that the cowboys in the company will not run wild. This is the approach most US in-house lawyers feel is required for their company's operations and sales teams and is generally designed to help avoid criminal liability.

The second approach focuses training on ethical values and is more prevalent in Europe where ethics and compliance are more designed to communicate a company's underlying corporate values in its operations. This approach anticipates that most employees are decent and law-abiding and will not knowingly engage in bribery and corruption. Additionally, you can never create enough rules to govern every situation and train each employee on every rule so a company must hire trustworthy people and give them sufficient information to make the correct ethical and compliant decision. Ms. Wrage characterizes the two different approaches as "ethics" vs. "values".

Both approaches have merit but both can catastrophically fail without the other components of an effective compliance program. For instance, having a "Gold Standard" Code of Compliance and Ethics alone is not enough. Although it was not brought down by a FCPA violation, the Enron Code of Ethics was viewed (at least at one time) as one of the strongest in the energy industry. And not to focus on US companies only, Siemens had one of the most robust Codes of Ethics for a European company before its multi-billion dollar (or euro - take your pick) fine and profit disgorgement. So the training on both of these company's "Gold Standard" codes of ethics did not turn out to be too helpful. But as pointed out by Kerri Grosslight, in her article "*Minimize Risk by Maximizing Accountability*" in Security Leadership, training is one of the key components.

So what should a company's training focus on in order to be "effective" under the Sentencing Guidelines? It appears that effective ethics and compliance training should emphasize both approaches. Americans are long taught what the rules are in whatever life they choose. They expect to be told what the rules will be so that they know where the line is drawn that they should not step over. Probably the single comment I have heard the most when putting on ethics and compliance training in the US is "Just tell me what I can and can't do". However, really effective training requires that employees be able to apply the rules to the incredibly wide and ever-changing situations which confront them in the real world. This is where communicating a company's values are important. In other words, how would your conduct look if it was plastered on You Tube the next week?

II. Types of Training

What type of training is most effective in the ethics and compliance arena? The consensus seems to be that there are three general approaches to ethics and compliance training which have been used successfully. The first is the most traditional and it is in-person classroom training. This gives employees an opportunity to see, meet and speak directly with a Compliance Officer, not an insignificant dynamic in the corporate environment. Such personal training also sends a strong message of commitment to compliance and ethics when training is held away from a corporation's home office. It gives employees the opportunity to interact with the Compliance Officer by asking questions which are relevant to markets and locations outside the United States. Lastly, it can also lead to confidential discussions after such in-person training.

An important part of in-person training is the opportunity to interact with the audience through Questions & Answers (Q&A). There are a couple different approaches to Q&A. The first is to solicit questions from the audience. However, many employees are reluctant, for a variety of different reasons, to raise their hands and ask questions in front of others. This can be overcome by soliciting written questions on cards or note pads. A second technique is to lead the audience through hypothetical examples in which the audience is broken down into small (up to 5 people) groups to discuss a situation and propose a response.

The second approach is on-line training. Rick Chapman, Assistant General Counsel for Halliburton in its Compliance & Ethics Practice Group, has said that online training is one of several training approaches used by Halliburton in ethics and compliance training. On-line training can be a helpful adjunct to live training because it can permeate a globally distributed organization and lends itself to automatic recordkeeping, tickling, and expiration management. He discussed this approach and its use by Halliburton to enable it to "effectively reach every employee at Halliburton worldwide" in *Ethisphere Magazine, June 7, 2007 "Expert Corner"*. Ethics and compliance courses are tailored to different categories of Halliburton employees and provided in multiple languages to ensure that all Halliburton employees will participate in ethics and compliance related learning activities at least once every two years by taking our general ethics and compliance training and/or issue-specific courses such as FCPA.

A third option has been suggested in *Wrageblog*. It is a combination of live in-person training followed by a live Q&A session filmed. Such a program can then be shown at other company offices around the world. Such a presentation should be lead in-person by a Compliance Officer who can follow up the filmed presentation by conducting a Q&A teleconference with the Compliance staff in the company's home office. *Wrageblog* believes that this approach can be a "very robust and inexpensive way to reach a large number of employees with a clear, tailored and forceful compliance message."

All three ethics and compliance training approaches should be coordinated and both the attendance and result recorded for the combined approach, online training and traditional training for all types of employees in all countries. Results can be tabulated through short questionnaires immediately following the training and bench-marked through more comprehensive interviewing of selected training participants to determine overall effectiveness.

Whatever approach is used, one of the critical factors is the length of time of the training session. While lawyers and ethics and compliance professionals can (sometimes) sit through 8 hours of such training, it is almost impossible to keep the attention of business and operations employees for such a length of time. The presentation must be kept to a manageable length and number of PowerPoint slides before eyes start to glaze over. My experience in all types of legal and compliance training has led me to believe that 3 hours is about the maximum length of in-person training which can hold the attention of business and operations employees for ethics and compliance training. For on-line training I would suggest a maximum length of one hour.

III. The Opening

As noted in Section I, a company's ethics and compliance training may well comprise several different audiences and different cultures around the globe. Top notch training should be able to reach all of the learners at such training sessions. One way to do so is to grab the audience's attention early by demonstrating the commitment of top management to ethics and compliance and make clear to each audience member how compliance laws such as the FCPA pertain directly to them. In his blog, the *FCPA Professor* has put forward a suggestion in his posting, "FCPA - The First Few Minutes" by proposing that an FCPA training session begin with an opening such as:

> "Today, I will be talking about a U.S. law that applies to all of you - regardless of whether you are in the sales and marketing department, the executive office suite, the finance and audit department, or the logistics department. This law can cover a wide range of payments the company makes, or could make, either directly or indirectly, in doing business or seeking business in foreign markets. Your understanding of this law and how it may relate to your specific job function will best ensure that the company remains compliant with this law and is able to achieve its business objectives."

Another technique to get the attention of the audience simply might be remind the them that hardly anyone looks good in a prison-orange jumpsuit and that you are here to present training to keep them out of such clothing.

IV. The End of the Day

At the end of the day, an effective training program will incorporate all learning tools available to reach the widest target audience possible. An individual's understanding of the rules is always important but it should be grounded in a company's ethical corporate culture. Coupled together, the Approaches listed in Section I, together with types of training discussed in Section II, should embolden employees to make the right decision even if they cannot remember a specific rule governing a situation. More importantly, such effective training provides knowledge about what an employee can and cannot do when confronted by those 'grey areas' that exist in the real world of international business.

Who Does Your Chief Compliance Officer Report To?

Posted June 12, 2010

There is an ongoing debate in the compliance arena as to whom a Chief Compliance Officer (CCO) should report. Should the CCO report to the Board of Directors or appropriate Board committee such as an Audit Committee or Compliance Committee? Or can a CCO report to a company's General Counsel (GC) but have access to the Board of Directors for periodic, but no less than annual, reporting? Is there any specific guidance from the Foreign Corrupt Practices Act (FCPA) or any of the US government interpretations such as the US Sentencing Guidelines, Deferred Prosecution Agreement (DPA) to which the Department of Justice (DOJ) and recalcitrant companies have entered into or Opinion Releases? Is one approach more right or more wrong than the other?

US companies are reported to take both approaches. A recent survey released by the Society of Corporate Compliance and Ethics (SCCE), entitled "*The Relationship Between the Board of Directors and the Compliance and Ethics Officer*" dated April 2010, reported that of the publicly traded companies reporting only 41% had their CCO report directly to the Board of Directors. If the CCO did not report to the Board of Directors, the survey found such position could report to not only the GC but also the Chief Financial Officer (CFO) and other senior level positions within a company. The report concluded with two perspectives from its findings. First that as the proposed change in the US Sentencing Guidelines would require "a direct" relationship between a CCO and a Board of Directors, most publicly traded companies do not meet this obligation. Second, many compliance reports are "heavily vetted" before they are delivered to the Board of Directors so that it may be hard to for a Board to garner a true picture of a company's compliance program.

I. US Sentencing Guidelines

Under the 2010 Amendments to the US Sentencing Guidelines which are now proposed to Congress, §8B2.1 (b)(2)(C) requires:

> Specific individual(s) within the organization shall be delegated day-to-day operational responsibility for the compliance and ethics program. Individual(s) with operational responsibility shall report periodically to high-level personnel and, as appropriate, to the governing authority, or an appropriate subgroup of the governing authority, on the effectiveness of the compliance and ethics program. To carry out such operational responsibility, such individual(s) shall be given adequate resources, appropriate authority, and direct access to the governing authority or an appropriate subgroup of the governing authority.

Commentators have weighed in on this amendment. In a recent White Paper entitled "*U.S. Sentencing Commission Amends Requirements for an Effective Compliance and Ethics Program*", the law firm of Gibson, Dunn and Crutcher noted that this amendment "could be problematic for corporations that vest overall responsibility for compliance in a senior member of management" such as the GC, while having operational responsibility of the company's compliance function detailed to a subordinate to the GC. They raised the concern that such a reporting structure might allow the GC to act as a "filter in deciding which conduct warrants reporting" to the Board of Directors, if the CCO reported. This would also imply there was a problem if a GC, rather than Board of Directors, performed an annual evaluation or in some other manner controlled the actions of the CCO.

II. Opinion Release 04-02

Through the mechanism of the Opinion Release 04-02 the DOJ may have provided prior guidance. The Opinion Release dealt with certain Requestors which were desired in order to acquire a business that had admitted to FCPA violations. As part of the proposed purchase of this "Newco", the Requestors agreed that this Newco would adopt a rigorous anti-corruption compliance code which would include the following element:

> (B) The assignment to one or more independent senior Newco corporate officials, who shall report *directly* to the Compliance Committee of the Audit Committee of the Board of Directors, of responsibility for the implementation and oversight of compliance with policies, standards, and procedures established in accordance with Newco's Compliance Code; [emphasis supplied]

III. Industry Debates

There has been debate in the FCPA compliance world as to what this requirement specifies. At the recent Compliance Week 2010 Annual Conference, a panel consisting of representatives from the US Sentencing Commission indicated that they believed that this section only required that CCOs have *access* to a company's

Board of Directors. Such a requirement could be fulfilled through a reporting structure whereby a CCO reported to a GC but had access to report to the Board of Directors, even if the CCO went to the Board of Directors with the GC present, such as reporting structure was in compliance with the proposed Sentencing Guidelines.

However, at the same conference, Assistant Attorney General, Criminal Division for the Department of Justice, Lanny Breuer said that a CCO should have *direct* access to a company's Board of Directors suggesting that the CCO not have to report through a GC but report directly to the Board. Breuer opined that the change in the Sentencing Guidelines implies that the CCO should now report directly to the Board of Directors and not through another person, whether the GC, CFO, Head of Internal Audit or any other person in an organization.

For yet a third perspective at the same conference, the question was put to a panel of members who sit on various Boards of Directors on multi-national US corporations, they responded that, as Board members, they only wanted the information to come to them so they could fulfill their obligations as Board members, they were not too concerned how it was presented to them or who did so. Further they were not concerned who the CCO reported to or which company officer or employee in the corporate structure evaluated the CCO.

A recent webcast by the firm of Ernst and Young further delineated this dichotomy. When posed the question of to whom should the CCO report to; either directly to the Board or the GC, panelists Brian Loughman and Jeff Taylor both indicated that it was important for the CCO to report directly to the Board. Such a reporting structure made a much more positive impression on the Board (Loughman) and that less filter of the CCO's information gave a stronger message to the Board (Taylor) than if the CCO reported through the GC. Loughman added that the change in the Sentencing Guidelines mandated this reporting structure. However, panelist Amy Hawkes responded that she did not believe the issue of who the CCO reported to was as important if there the appropriate 'tone at the top' by the Board. By this she explained that if the Board was committed to a compliance culture, it did not matter whether the CCO reported directly to the Board or to the Board through the GC.

This direct reporting approach is utilized by Halliburton, to which I posed the following question, "Who does the Chief Compliance Officer report to in your Company and why does your company utilize this approach?" Susan Ponce, Senior Vice President and Chief Ethics and Compliance Officer of Halliburton responded, "*At Halliburton, the Chief Ethics and Compliance Officer reports directly to the company's Board of Directors, advising both the Audit Committee and the full Board on all matters relating to legal compliance issues. We structured the CEC Office that way in order to leave no doubt that the CECO has direct, independent and unfettered access to our Board and support from board members and our senior executives.*"

The answer to the initial question posed appears to have two correct responses. The guidelines and debate goes both ways. The key is in the actual reporting. As long as the CCO reports on a regular basis to the Board, both lines of authority are appear to be acceptable.

So which approach does your company utilize?

What's in a Name under the FCPA?

Posted November 15, 2010

What is in a name? The terms agent, reseller and distributor are sometimes used interchangeably in the business world. However, in the legal world they usually have distinct definitions. An agent can be generally defined as is a person who is authorized to act on behalf of another to create a legal relationship with a Third Party.

Agent

An agent can also be a person who makes introductions and generally facilitates relationships between the seller of goods or services and the end-using buyer. Such an agent usually receives some type of percentage of the final sale as his commission. An in-country national agent is often required in most Middle East and Far East countries.

Reseller

A reseller can be generally defined as a company or individual that sells goods to an end-using buyer. A reseller does not take title and thereby own the goods; the reseller is usually a conduit from the seller to the end-using buyer. A reseller usually receives a flat commission for his services, usually between 5-10% of the final purchase price. This format is often used in the software and hardware industries.

Distributor

A distributor can be generally defined as a company

or individual who purchases a product from an original equipment manufacturer (OEM) and then independently sells that product to an end user. A distributor takes title, physical possession and owns the products. The distributor then sells the product again to an end-using purchaser. The distributor usually receives the product at some discount from the OEM and then is free to set his price at any amount above what he paid for the product. A distributor is often used by the US manufacturing industry to act as a sales force outside the US.

The landscape of the Foreign Corrupt Practices Act (FCPA) is littered with cases involving both agents and resellers where they are the most clearly acting as representatives of the companies whose goods or services they sell for in foreign countries. However, many US businesses believe that the legal differences between agent/reseller and distributor insulates them from FCPA liability should the conduct of the distributor violate the Act. They believe that as the distributor takes title and physical possession of the product, the legal risk of ownership has shifted to the distributor. If the goods are damaged or destroyed, the loss will be the distributor's not the US business which manufactured the product. Under this same analysis, many US companies believe that the FCPA risk has also shifted from the US company to the foreign distributor. However, such belief is sorely miss-placed.

As almost everyone knows, the FCPA prohibits payments to foreign officials to obtain or retain business or secure an improper business advantage. But many US companies view distributors as different from other types of sales representatives such as company sales representatives, agents, resellers or even joint venture partners, for the purposes of FCPA liability. However, the Department of Justice (DOJ) takes the position that a US company's FCPA responsibilities extend to the conduct of a wide range of third parties, including the aforementioned company sales representatives, agents, resellers, joint venture partners but also distributors. No US company can ignore signs that its distributors may be violating the FCPA. Company management cannot engage in *conscious avoidance* to the activities of a distributor that the company has put into a business position favorable to engaging in FCPA violations. Court interpretation of the FCPA has held that it is applicable where conduct violative of the Act is used to "to obtain or retain business or secure an improper business advantage" which can cover almost any kind of advantage, including indirect monetary advantage even as nebulous as reputational advantage.

This scenario played out in China from 1997 to 2005 through AGA Medical Corporation (AGA). The Minnesota-based firm manufactured products used to treat congenital heart defects. To boost is China sales, AGA worked through its Chinese distributor. AGA sold products at a discounted rate to its Chinese distributor. This distributor then took some of the difference between his price from the equipment manufacturer AGA and the price he sold the equipment to Chinese hospitals for and paid corrupt payments to Chinese doctors to have them direct their government-owned hospitals to purchase AGA's products. Its sales in China for the period were about $13.5 million. The Chinese distributor was found to have paid bribes in China of at least $460,000 to doctors in government-owned hospitals and patent-office officials. In 2008, AGA agreed to pay a $2 million criminal penalty and enter into a Deferred Prosecution Agreement (DPA) with the DOJ to settle FCPA violations.

The same game was played by a Volvo subsidiary, Volvo Construction Equipment International (VCEI) when it used a Tunisian distributor to facilitate additional sales of its products to Iraq. VCEI reduced its prices to enable the distributor to make the illegal payments based on bogus after-sales service fees. Volvo's 2008 settlement with the Securities and Exchange Commission (SEC) included an agreement permanently enjoining it from future violations of Sections, ordering it to disgorge $7,299,208 in profits plus $1,303,441 in pre-judgment interest, and to pay a civil penalty of $4,000,000. In addition to this fine imposed by the SEC, Volvo also paid a $7,000,000 penalty pursuant to a DPA with the DOJ.

So what is in a name? Do we simply look to Shakespeare and his immortal words, "What's in a name? That which we call a rose; By any other name would smell as sweet." Unfortunately I do not think the answer is quite so ethereal. It is more down to earth. If it walks like a duck and quacks like a duck, it probably is a duck. If you have a distributor, it must be subjected to the same FCPA scrutiny and management as an agent, reseller or joint venture partner.

Real Estate, Trial Lawyers and FCPA Compliance

Posted May 7, 2010

What do real estate, trial lawyers and Foreign Corrupt Practice Act (FCPA) compliance have in common? One of the maxims you hear about the real estate business, even in the depressed market over the past 18 months, is that the three most important things are: (1) location, (2) location and (3) location. This commentator was a trial lawyer, on the civil side, for about 18 years of his legal career and it was drilled into him that the three most important things a trial lawyer brings to a lawsuit are: (1) venue, (2) venue and (3) venue.

It was then with some interest that this commentator saw a video on the Project Counsel website (a great resource, they not only blog with summaries of speakers at significant legal conferences but also present interviews with conference speakers on its website), where Project Counsel Managing Director Greg Bufithis, interviewed Tim Parkman, Managing Director of Lessons Learned Ltd., a UK entity which assists companies in implementing compliance and ethics programs. In response to a query by Mr. Bufithis on what was the single most important item for a business which is implementing a compliance and ethics program, Mr. Parkman responded that there were three: "(1) senior management, (2) senior management and (3) senior management."

Parkman explained his logic behind this statement of triumviratism is because employees will pick up on the differences between what senior management says versus the actions that they might take with regard to compliance and ethics. He cited that a prime example of this is what policy does a company take to punish those employees who may engage in unethical and non-compliant behavior in order to meet company revenue targets versus what rewards are handed out to those employees who integrate such ethical and compliant behavior into their individual work practices going forward?

A clear example of this is in the area of annual bonuses. Does your company have, as a component of its bonus compensation plan, a part dedicated to compliance and ethics? If so, how is this component measured and then administered? There is very little in the corporate world that an employee notices more than what goes into the calculation of their bonuses. If a company sets expectations early in the year and then follows through when annual bonuses are released, it can send a powerful message to employees regarding the seriousness with which compliance is taken at the company. There is nothing like putting your money where your mouth is for people to stand up and take notice.

Parkman goes on to say that if you have an employee who meets, or exceeds all his sales targets, but does so in a manner which is opposite to the company's stated compliance and ethics values, employees will watch and see how that employee is treated. Is that employee rewarded with a large bonus? Is that employee promoted or are the employee's violations of the company's compliance and ethics policies swept under the carpet? If the employee is rewarded, or in any way not sanctioned for unethical or non-compliant behavior, it will be noticed and other employees will act accordingly.

In the energy industry, (and probably lots of other

industries) there is the following archetypal story, it is usually told about a Regional Manager in the Far East or Middle East who is alleged to have said some along the following lines, "If I violate the Code of Conduct I may or may not get caught. If I get caught I may or may not be disciplined. But if don't make my revenue numbers for two quarters I will be fired". If such a story is allowed to percolate throughout the company, employees will feel that all that matters is hitting their revenue targets, not acting in an ethical and compliant manner. Only senior management can directly speak to this issue and senior management must make clear that "hitting the numbers" in a manner which is antithetical to the company's compliance and ethics program is not acceptable. But this must be done in both words ***and*** actions.

So does your company only "talk the talk or does it also walk the walk?"

The Board of Directors and FCPA Compliance

Posted August 10, 2010

Where does "Tone at the Top" start? With any public and most private US companies, it is at the Board of Directors. But what is the role of a company's Board in Foreign Corrupt Practices Act (FCPA) compliance? We start with several general statements about the role of a Board in US companies. First a Board should not engage in management but should engage in oversight of a Chief Executive Officer (CEO) and senior management. The Board does this through asking hard questions, risk assessment and identification.

In a recent panel discussion to the Texas TriCities Chapter of the National Association of Corporate Directors, panelist Mike Tankersley, Executive Vice President and General Counsel of CSG Investment, provided some of his more anecdotal thoughts on the Board role. His initial thoughts were that the role of a Board is to "keep really bad things from happening to the Company" and added that the role is to "make sure the Company exists." Tankersley believes that one of the ways a Board can assist a company to make money is by giving oversight to risk management. He opined this can be accomplished through an Audit Committee or a Compliance Committee.

In a recent White Paper, entitled "Risk Intelligence Governance - *A Practical Guide for Boards*" the firm of

Deloitte & Touche laid out six general principles to help guide Boards in the area of risk governance. These six areas can be summarized as follows:

- Define the Board's Role - There must be a mutual understanding between the Board, CEO and senior management of the Board's responsibilities.
- Foster a culture of risk management - All stakeholders should understand the risks involved and manage such risks accordingly.
- Incorporate risk management directly into a strategy - Oversee the design and implementation of risk evaluation and analysis.
- Help define the company's appetite for risk - All stakeholders need to understand the company's appetite or lack thereof for risk.
- How to execute the risk management process - The risk management process maintaining an approach that is continually monitored and had continuing accountability.
- How to benchmark and evaluate the process - Systems need to be installed which allow for evaluation and modifying the risk management process as more information becomes available or facts or assumptions change.

All of these factors can be easily adapted to FCPA compliance and ethics risk management oversight. Initially it must be important that the Board receive direct access to such information on a company's policies on this issue. The Board must have quarterly or semi-annual reports from a company's Chief Compliance Officer (CCO) to either the Audit Committee or the Compliance Committee. This commentator recommends that a Board create a Compliance Committee as an Audit Committee may more appropriately deal with financial audit issues. A Compliance Committee can devote itself exclusively to non-financial compliance, such as FCPA compliance. The Board's oversight role should be to receive such regular reports on the structure of the company's compliance program, its actions and self-evaluations. From this information the Board can give oversight to any modifications to managing FCPA risk that should be implemented.

There is one other issue regarding the Board and risk management, including FCPA risk management, which should be noted. It appears that the Securities and Exchange Commission (SEC) desires Boards to take a more active role in overseeing the management of risk within a company. The SEC has promulgated Reg SK 407 under which each company must make a disclosure regarding the Board's role in risk oversight which "may enable investors to better evaluate whether the board is exercising appropriate oversight of risk." If this disclosure is not made, it could be a securities law violation and subject the company which fails to make it to fines, penalties or profit disgorgement.

Board Members and Prudent Discharge of Duties under the FCPA

Posted August 24, 2010

Monday's FCPA Blog post wrote about what it called a "compliance donnybrook" inside the company China North East Petroleum (NPE). The facts of this melee are straightforward, in July 2010, the head of the Board of Director's Audit Committee Robert Bruce, communicated to his fellow directors that he believed the company needed an investigation to make sure it had not violated the Foreign Corrupt Practices Act's (FCPA) anti-bribery provisions and did so in a letter detailing his reasons for making this request. As reported by the FCPA Blog, Mr. Bruce stated, in part "I strongly believe that substantial additional investigation is required in order for the Company and/or the members of the board to be confident that . . . the Company has not made payments to government officials as proscribed by the U.S. Foreign Corrupt Practices Act."

The Chairman of the Board of Directors of NPE, Mr. Edward Rule, responded by declining this request for a FCPA investigation, which Mr. Bruce had suggested be led by an outside law firm with a strong FCPA background. Mr. Rule noted that such an investigation "could last as long as a full year and cost the Company as much as several millions of dollars" and could even lead to the delisting the company from the NYSE Amex. Mr. Rule ended his letter by noting "the course of action you recommend that the

Board pursue seems at odds with the ***prudent discharge*** of duties to the shareholders".

This final sentence caught the attention of the FCPA Compliance and Ethics Blog. What are the obligations of a Board member regarding the FCPA? Are the obligations of the Audit Committee under the FCPA at odds with a director's "*prudent discharge* of duties to shareholders"? Do the words *prudent discharge* even appear anywhere in the FCPA? My search into answers for the first two questions began with a recent EthicsPoint webinar, entitled "Reporting to the Board on Your Compliance Program: New Guidance and Good Practices", where attorneys Rebecca Walker and Jeffery Kaplan, of the law firm of Kaplan and Walker, explored these and other issues.

Mr. Kaplan pointed to the US Sentencing Guidelines and Department of Justice (DOJ) Prosecution Standards for guidance as to the obligations of a company's Board regarding FCPA compliance. Under the US Sentencing Guidelines, Ms. Walker said that the Board must exercise reasonable oversight on the effectiveness of a company's compliance program. Ms. Walker said that the DOJ Prosecution Standards posed the following queries: (1) Do the Directors exercise independent review of a company's compliance program; and (2) Are Directors provided information sufficient to enable the exercise of independent judgment?

As to the specific role of 'Best Practices' in the area of general compliance and ethics, Ms. Walker looked to Delaware corporate law for guidance. She cited to the case of *Stone v. Ritter* for the proposition that "a duty to attempt in good faith to assure that a corporate information and reporting system, which the board concludes is adequate exists." From the case of *In re Walt Disney Company Derivative Litigation*, she drew the principle that directors should follow the best practices in the area of ethics and compliance.

In a recent Compliance Week article, Melissa Aguilar examined the duties of Board members regarding FCPA compliance. The conclusions of several of the FCPA experts that Ms. Aguilar interviewed for the article were that companies which have not yet had any FCPA issues rise up to the Board level are usually the ones which are the most at risk. Albert Vondra, a partner with PricewaterhouseCoopers stated that such companies "don't have the incentive to spend the resources or take the rigorous approach to their anti-compliance programs. Their attitude is, 'We've got it covered,' but they don't." Richard Cassin, managing partner of Cassin Law, stated that there must be written records demonstrating that the audit committee and that the board members asked questions and received answers regarding FCPA compliance issues. Such documentation demonstrates the Board members have "fulfilled their fiduciary obligations," Cassin says.

Board failure to heed this warning can lead to serious consequences. David Stuart, a senior attorney with Cravath Swaine & Moore, noted that FCPA compliance issues can lead to personal liability for directors, as both the Securities and Exchange Commission (SEC) and DOJ have been "very vocal about their interest in identifying the highest-level individuals within the organization who are responsible for the tone, culture, or weak internal controls that may contribute to, or at least fail to prevent, bribery and corruption". He added that based upon the SEC's enforcement action against two senior executives at Nature's Sunshine, "Under certain circumstances, I could see the SEC invoking the same provisions against audit committee members—for instance, for failing to oversee implementation of a compliance program to mitigate risk of bribery".

What does all of this mean for Messers Bruce, Rule and the rest of the Board members of NPE? It should mean quite a bit. The DOJ has made it clear that it expects 'best practices' when it comes to FCPA compliance. In the case of NPE, the head of the Board's Audit Committee has requested an independent FCPA compliance investigation, to be effected by an outside firm. The Chairman of the Board of Directors has rejected this request because (1) it might take up to a year; (2) it might cost too much money AND fulfilling its FCPA obligation "seems at odds with the *prudent discharge* of duties to the shareholders". The head of the Audit Committee resigned over this rejection.

Alas, there is no reference to *prudent discharge* in the FCPA itself. However, if I were a remaining member of the Board of NPE, I might well think more than twice about my *prudent discharge* of duties to the shareholders as both the DOJ and SEC now might well wish to look into this matter under a Board's *prudent discharge* of duties under the FCPA.

Provenance in the Supply Chain: Transparency and Accountability under the FCPA and Bribery Act

Posted October 20, 2010

In the October 2010 issue of the Harvard Business Review there is a Spotlight article on "*The Transparent Supply Chain*". In this article, author Stephen New discusses the evolution in Supply Chain from opaqueness to transparency and focuses on the "quality, safety, ethics and environmental impact" of the Supply Chain on the triumvirate of companies, customers and government. New terms this information as "*Provenance*" and this is relevant both up and down the Supply Chain.

New points out that customers are becoming increasingly concerned with not only the authenticity of the goods they purchased but also the ethics of how the goods were manufactured in the Supply Chain. Companies have long been concerned with the quality of goods and services they receive from their Supply Chain vendors and tracking this information can provide assurances of high quality control. Increasingly the third prong of the triumvirate, the government, is now requesting such information and such transparency in the area of anti-corruption and anti-bribery compliance.

Under both the US Foreign Corrupt Practices Act (FCPA) and the UK Bribery Act, it is now critical that companies bring their Supply Chain vendors into their overall compliance programs. This message has been given renewed emphasis with the recent report in the FCPA Blog (and others) that the freight forwarder Panalpina may be close to a settlement with the Department of Justice (DOJ) over its FCPA violations. One of the major fallouts from the Panalpina case was the ripple effect through the energy industry, after the initial disclosure that Panalpina had paid bribes in Nigeria, while working as a freight forwarder to Vetco Grey. Other energy companies which had used Panalpina to bring goods and materials into Nigeria came under DOJ investigation for possible FCPA violations; these other companies were reported to include Transocean, GlobalSantaFe Corp., Noble Corp., Nabors Industries, Tidewater, Schlumberger, Shell and Global Industries.

In addition to the effect of the Panalpina matter, the new released UK Bribery Act Consultation Guidance specifically lists due diligence on Supply Chain vendors as a key component of its anti-bribery and anti-corruption *best practices*. Principle Six of the Guidance states, "*The commercial organisation has due diligence policies and procedures which cover all parties to a business relationship, including the organisation's* ***supply chain****, agents and intermediaries, all forms of joint venture and similar relationships and all markets in which the commercial organisation does business*." This means that due diligence should be engaged to establish whether individuals or other organizations involved in key decisions have a reputation for bribery and whether anyone associated with them is being investigated, prosecuted, or has been convicted or debarred for bribery or related offences. Consideration should be given to the risks associated with politically exposed persons where the proposed business relationship involves, or is linked to, a prominent public office holder. Lastly, a review of Supply Chain vendors own compliance programs should be effected.

All of this brings us back to New's article and his terminology of "*Provenance*". In the FCPA/UK Bribery Act context this should be defined as full transparency and accountability in all areas of due diligence and the relationship after the contract is signed with the supplier. A company should, on a periodic basis of not less than every three years, conduct rigorous compliance audits of its operations with its Supply Chain vendors. These audits would include, but not be limited to, detailed audits of the Supply Chain vendor's books and records, with specific attention to payments and commissions to agents, consultants, contractors, and subcontractors with responsibilities that include interactions with foreign officials. This compliance audit should include interviews with employees, consultants, agents, contractors, subcontractors and joint venture partners. Lastly, a review of the FCPA compliance training provided to the Supply Chain vendor should be included.

Just as *Provenance* is the new by-word in Supply Chain management in the Harvard Business Review; transparency and accountability in the area of anti-corruption and anti-bribery should have the same urgency to companies' subject to the FCPA and/or UK Bribery Act. The Panalpina case is a stark reminder of the need for continued diligence, before and after the contract is signed, in the compliance arena.

The FCPA Audit for Supply Chain Vendors

Posted December 16, 2010

An audit for adherence to Foreign Corrupt Practices Act (FCPA) compliance requirements is becoming more standard as a *best practice* in the management of business relationships with third party vendors which work with a company through the supply chain. In several recent settlements of enforcement actions through both Deferred Prosecution Agreements (DPA), e.g. Panalpina, and Non-Prosecution Agreements (NPA), e.g. RAE Systems Inc., the Department of Justice (DOJ) has stated that one of the current *best practices* of a FCPA compliance program includes the right to conduct audits of the books and records of the agents, business partners, suppliers or contractors to ensure compliance with the foregoing. Many companies have yet to begin their audit process for FCPA compliance on vendors in their supply chain. This posting will explore some of the issues involved in auditing such business partners.

I. Right to Audit

Initially it should be noted that a company must obtain the right to audit for FCPA compliance in its contract with any third party vendor in the supply chain. Such an audit right should be a part of a company's standard terms and conditions. A sample clause could include language such as the following:

The vendor shall permit, upon the request of and at

sole discretion of the Company,, audits by independent auditors acceptable to Company, and agree that such auditors shall have full and unrestricted access to, and to conduct reviews of, all records related to the work performed for, or services or equipment provided to, Company, and to report any violation of any of the United States Foreign Corrupt Practices Act, UK Bribery Act or any other applicable laws and regulations, with respect to:

a) the effectiveness of existing compliance programs and codes of conduct;

b) the origin and legitimacy of any funds paid to Company;

c) its books, records and accounts, or those of any of its subsidiaries, joint ventures or affiliates, related to work performed for, or services or equipment provided to, Company;

d) all disbursements made for or on behalf of Company; and

e) all funds received from Company in connection with work performed for, or services or equipment provided to, Company.

II. Structure of the Audit

In the December 2010 issue of the ***Industrial Engineer Magazine***, authors Tariq Aldowaisan and Elaf Ashkanani discussed the audit program utilized by the Kuwait National Petroleum Company for its supply chain vendors. Although the focus of these audits is not to review FCPA compliance, the referenced audits are designed to detect and report incidents of non-compliance, which would also be the goal of a FCPA compliance audit. Utilizing ISO 19011 as the basis to set the parameters of an audit, the authors define an audit as a "systematic, independent and documented process for obtaining audit evidence and evaluating it objectively to determine the extent to which the audit criteria are fulfilled." The authors list three factors, which they believe contribute to a successful audit: (1) an effective audit program which specifies all necessary activities for the audit; (2) having competent auditors in place; and (3) an organization that is committed to being audited. In a webinar hosted by Securities Docket, entitled "*Follow the Money: Using Technology to Find Fraud or Defend Financial Investigations*", noted fraud examiner expert Tracy Coenen described the process as one to (1) capture the data; (2) analyze the data; and (3) report on the data.

There is no one specific list of transactions or other items which should be audited. However, some of the audit best practices would suggest the following:

- Review of contracts with supply chain vendors to confirm that the appropriate FCPA compliance terms and conditions are in place.
- Determine that actual due diligence took place on the third party vendor.
- Review FCPA compliance training program; both the substance of the program and attendance records.
- Does the third party vendor have a hotline or any other reporting mechanism for allegations of compliance violations? If so how are such reports maintained? Review any reports of compliance violations or issues that arose through anonymous reporting, hotline or any other reporting mechanism.
- Does the third party vendor have written employee discipline procedures? If so have any employees been disciplined for any compliance violations? If yes review all relevant files relating to any such violations to determine the process used and the

outcome reached.

- Review employee expense reports for employees in high risk positions or high risk countries.
- Testing for gifts, travel and entertainment which were provided to, or for, foreign governmental officials.
- Review the overall structure of the third party vendor's compliance program. If the company has a designated compliance officer to whom, and how, does that compliance officer report? How is the third party vendor's compliance program designed to identify risks and what has been the result of any so identified?
- Review a sample of employee commission payments and determine if they follow the internal policy and procedure of the third party vendor.
- With regard to any petty cash activity in foreign locations, review a sample of activity and apply analytical procedures and testing. Analyze the general ledger for high-risk transactions and cash advances and apply analytical procedures and testing.

III. Conclusion

As noted the above list is not exhaustive. For instance, there could be an audit focus on internal controls or segregation of duties. Any organization which audits a business partner in its supply chain should consult with legal, audit, financial and supply chain professionals to determine the full scope of the audit and a thorough and complete work plan should be created based upon all these professional inputs. At the conclusion of an audit, an audit report should be issued. This audit report should detail incidents of non-compliance with the FCPA compliance program and recommendations for improvements. Any reported incidents of non-compliance should reference the basis of any incidents of non-compliance such as contractual clauses, legal requirement or company policies.

Establishing Relationships with Foreign Business Partners - Due Diligence, Due Diligence and then Due Diligence

Posted February 22, 2010

There are several critical components in the selection, use and retention of any Foreign Business Partner, such as agents, resellers, joint venture partners or distributors. In view of the critical risks a US Company must manage when entering into a relationship with a Foreign Business Partner, the US Company should, prior to establishing the relationship, kick off the risk management process by initiating thorough due diligence on the proposed Foreign Business Partner. The due diligence process should contain, at a minimum, inquiries into the following areas:

- **Need for the relationship with a Foreign Business Partner:** The Company Business Team or Business Person should articulate the business case for the proposed Foreign Business Partner relationship. This must be approved by management before it goes to legal or compliance for review.
- **Credentials:** List the critical reasons for selection of the proposed Foreign Business Partner. This should include a discussion of the business partner's background and experience.
- **Ownership Structure**: Describe whether

the proposed Foreign Business Partner is a government or state-owned entity, and the nature of its relationship(s) with local, regional and governmental bodies. Are there any members of the business partner related, by blood, to governmental officials?

- **Financial Qualifications:** Describe the financial stability of, and all capital to be provided by, the proposed Foreign Business Partner. Obtain financial records, audited for 3 to 5 years, if available.
- **Personnel:** Determine whether the Foreign Business Partner will be providing personnel, particularly whether any of the employees are government officials. Obtain the names and titles of those who will provide services to the US Company.
- **Physical Facilities:** Describe what physical facilities will be provided by the Foreign Business Partner. Who will provide the necessary capital for their upkeep?
- **Reputation:** Describe the business reputation of the proposed Foreign Business Partner in its geographic and industry-sector markets.

These due diligence inquiries are required under the US Federal Sentencing Guidelines and the guidance offered by the Department of Justice (DOJ) Opinion Releases and the publicly released Plea Agreements and Deferred Prosecution Agreements (DPA) entered into by US companies who admit to violating the Foreign Corrupt Practices Act (FCPA). This due diligence should be recorded and maintained by the US Company for review, if required, by a governmental agency. Some of the due diligence can be handled by the US Company's in-house legal and/or compliance groups. However, it is recommended that for any high risk Foreign Business Partner, an outside forensic auditing firm and outside legal counsel be retained to conduct the due diligence investigations. This brings a level of expertise usually not available within a corporation plus an outside perspective less susceptible to in-company business pressures.

After this initial inquiry is concluded the US Company should move forward to perform a background check on a prospective Foreign Business Partner by using the following resources:

- **References:** Obtain and contact a list of business references.
- **Embassy Check:** Obtain information regarding the intended business partner from the local US Embassy, including an International Company Profile Report.
- **Compliance Verification:** Determine if the Foreign Business Partner, and those persons within the Foreign Business Partner who will be providing services to the US Company, have reviewed or received FCPA training.
- **Foreign Country Check:** Have an independent third party, such as a law firm; investigate the business partner in its home country to determine compliance with its home country's laws, licensing requirements and regulations.
- **Cooperation and Attitude:** One of the most important inquiries is not legal but based upon the response and cooperation of the Foreign Business Partner. Did the business partner object to any portion of the due diligence process? Did it object to the scope, coverage or purpose of the FCPA? In short, is the business partner a person or entity that the US Company is willing to stand up with under the FCPA?

After a company completes these due diligence steps, there should be a thorough review by the Board, or other dedicated Management Committee, on the qualifications of the proposed foreign business relationship partner. It is critical that the reviewing Committee is not subordinate to the US company's business unit which is responsible for the business transactions with the Foreign Business Partner. This review should examine the adequacy of due diligence performed in connection with the selection of overseas partners, as well as the Foreign Business Partner's selection of agents, subcontractors and consultants which will be used for business development on behalf of the US Company.

The steps listed herein do not include the use of, or continued management of, a Foreign Business Partner. These steps need to be taken by all US Companies entering into, or already engaged in, a relationship with Foreign Business Partners as the FCPA applies to all US Companies, whether public or private. Remember, due diligence, due diligence and once that has been completed; more due diligence.

Internal Review of a Proposed Foreign Business Partner

Posted March 4, 2010

In prior blogs, we explored how to rank Foreign Business Partners so that you can begin an appropriate due diligence process. We also explored what you might wish to investigate during the due diligence process. A Foreign Business Partner Review Committee should be established which is tasked with reviewing all the investigative due diligence and the Business Unit's case for partnering with the person or entity. The next area of review should of the proposed Foreign Business Partner's ethics and compliance program. Such a program should have, at a minimum, the following elements of a Foreign Corrupt Practices Act (FCPA) style compliance program in place.

- Your Foreign Business Partner should...
    - ◊ have a restriction on facilitation payments, gifts, entertainment and travel;
    - ◊ require proper accounting and invoicing;
    - ◊ have policies that flow down to any sub-vendors under the Foreign Business Partner

If the Foreign Business Partner's program does not meet your Company's, or the FCPA, standards you should require the implementation of a program that will meet those suggested in the US Sentencing Guidelines so that it will meet Department of Justice (DOJ) approval.

The next area of review by the Foreign Business Partner Review Committee is the proposed contract with the Foreign Business Partner. The contract must have compliance obligations stated in the formation documents, whether it is a simple agency or consulting agreement or a joint venture with several formation documents. All formation agreements should include representations that in all undertakings the Foreign Business Partner will make no payments of money, or anything of value, nor will such be offered, promised or paid, directly or indirectly, to any foreign officials, political parties, party officials, or candidates for public or political party office, to influence the acts of such officials, political parties, party officials, or candidates in their official capacity, to induce them to use their influence with a government to obtain or retain business or gain an improper advantage in connection with any business venture or contract in which the Company is a participant.

In addition to the above affirmative statement regarding conduct, you should have the following contractual clauses in your Foreign Business Partner contract.

- Indemnification: Full indemnification for any FCPA violation, including all costs for the underlying investigation.
- Cooperation: Require full cooperation with any ethics and compliance investigation, specifically including the review of Foreign Business Partner emails and bank accounts relating to your Company's use of the Foreign Business Partner.
- Material Breach of Contract: Any FCPA violation is made a material breach of contract, with no notice and opportunity to cure. Further such a finding will be the grounds for immediate cessation of all payments.
- No Sub-Vendors (without approval): The Foreign

Business Partner must agree that it will not hire an agent, subcontractor or consultant without the Company's prior written consent (to be based on adequate due diligence).

- Audit Rights: An additional key element of a contract between a US Company and a Foreign Business Partner should include the retention of audit rights. These audit rights must exceed the simple audit rights associated with the financial relationship between the parties and must allow a full review of all FCPA related compliance procedures such as those for meeting with foreign governmental officials and compliance related training.
- Acknowledgment: The Foreign Business Partner should specifically acknowledge the applicability of the FCPA to the business relationship as well as any country or regional anti-corruption or anti-bribery laws which apply to either the Foreign Business Partner or business relationship.
- On-going Training: Require that the top management of the Foreign Business Partner and all persons performing services on your behalf shall receive FCPA compliance training.
- Annual Certification: Require an annual certification stating that the Foreign Business Partner has not engaged in any conduct that violates the FCPA or any applicable laws, nor is it aware of any such conduct.
- Re-qualification: Require the Foreign Business Partner re-qualify as a business partner at a regular interval of no greater than every three years.

Engaging in due diligence of a proposed Foreign Business Partner is but one of the many steps required to approve a person or entity who will represent your

Company overseas, thereby creating a FCPA exposure. However, there are additional steps which you should employ internally in the Foreign Business Partner review process, some of which have been discussed above. Strong compliance terms and conditions are critical for the management of the relationship going forward. The Foreign Business Partner Review Committee must certify that the appropriate terms and conditions are in place to protect against a FCPA compliance violation and, should one occur, your Company can extricate itself immediately from doing business with such a Foreign Business Partner.

Maintaining a Relationship with a Foreign Business Partner after the Contract is signed - Monitor, Monitor and then Monitor

Posted March 9, 2010

In previous postings, we have shared our thoughts on other aspect of the Foreign Business Partner (foreign agents, reseller, distributors or any person/entity representing the company overseas) relationship including how to evaluate the Foreign Corrupt Practices Act (FCPA) compliance risk; how to perform due diligence on prospective Foreign Business Partners; how to internally evaluate the information obtained through such due diligence; and what compliance contract terms and conditions you should set for the Foreign Business Partners. In this posting, we will discuss the steps a US company must follow to implement a procedure to monitor the actions of a Foreign Business Partner going forward.

DPA Guidance

In its Deferred Prosecution Agreement (DPA) with the Monsanto Company for their FCPA violations, the Department of Justice (DOJ) provided some guidance on the continuing obligation to monitor Foreign Business Partners. In the Monsanto DPA, the DOJ agreed, after the initial due diligence and appropriate review were completed on Foreign Business Partners, for Monsanto to implement certain post contract procedures. These requirements to Monsanto can be used as guidelines as to what the DOJ will look for from other US companies who have entered into relationships with Foreign Business Partners; especially in the area of monitoring the Foreign Business Partner.

A US company should, on a periodic basis of not less than every three years, conduct rigorous compliance audits of its operations with the Foreign Business Partners. This monitoring would include, but not be limited to, detailed audits of their books and records, with specific attention to payments and commissions to agents, consultants, contractors, and subcontractors with responsibilities that include interactions with foreign officials and contributions to joint ventures. The compliance audit should include interviews with employees, consultants, agents, contractors, subcontractors and joint venture partners. Lastly, a review of the FCPA compliance training provided should be included.

Ongoing Oversight

In addition to the DOJ guidance provided in the Monsanto DPA, it is recommended that there be substantial involvement not only by the business unit most closely involved with the Foreign Business Partner, but also by Legal; Compliance and other departments which would assist in completing the functions as outlined by the Monsanto DPA. The most significant reason for maintaining a post-contract relationship is to ensure the business units remain engaged in the Foreign Business Partner process. This involvement can also include some of the following participation, the senior business Vice President (VP) for the region where the Foreign Business Partner operates should annually call upon the Foreign Business Partner, in-person, to review all of the prospective business proposals and concluded business transactions that the Foreign Business Partner has engaged in. This annual VP review must not take the place of a legal or compliance review but should focus on the relationship from the business perspective.

Managing the risk of a relationship with a Foreign Business Partner is one of the most critical aspects of a FCPA compliance program. The documented risk for the potential violation of the FCPA by a Foreign Business Partner to a US company is quite high. To engage a Foreign Business Partner, in a manner that properly assesses and manages the risk to and for a US company, requires a committee of time, money and substantial effort. However, with a compliance based risk management procedure in place, the risk can be properly managed and a foreign business relationship can be successful for all parties.

The Role of Human Resources in FCPA Compliance – Part I

Posted May 12, 2010

One sign of a mature Foreign Corrupt Practices Act (FCPA) compliance and ethics program is the extent to which a company's Human Resources (HR) Department is involved in implementing a solution. While many practitioners do not immediately consider HR as a key component of a FCPA compliance solution, it can be one of the lynch-pins in spreading a company's commitment to compliance throughout the employee base. HR can also be used to 'connect the dots' in many divergent elements of a FCPA compliance and ethics program. My next two postings will discuss the role of HR in such a program. The first installment will discuss training, employee evaluation, succession planning, hotlines and investigations. In the next posting, we will discuss background screening, doing 'more with less' and finally, what to do when the government comes calling.

Training

A key role for HR in any company is training. This has traditionally been in areas such as discrimination, harassment and safety, to name just a few, and based on this traditional role of HR in training this commentator would submit that it is a natural extension of HR's function to the area of FCPA compliance and ethics. There is a training requirement set forth in the US

Sentencing Guidelines. Companies are mandated to "*take reasonable steps to communicate periodically and in a practical manner its standards and procedures, and other aspects of the compliance and ethics program, to the individuals referred to in subdivision (B) by conducting effective training programs and otherwise disseminating information appropriate to such individuals' respective roles and responsibilities.*"

What type of training should HR utilize in the FCPA compliance and ethics arena? The consensus seems to be that there are three general approaches to ethics and compliance training which have been used successfully. The first is the most traditional and that is in-person classroom training. This gives employees an opportunity to see, meet and interact directly with the trainer, not an insignificant dynamic in the corporate environment. It can also lead to confidential discussions after such in-person training. All FCPA compliance and ethics training should be coordinated and both the attendance and results recorded. Results can be tabulated through short questionnaires immediately following the training and bench-marked through more comprehensive interviewing of selected training participants to determine overall effectiveness.

Employee Evaluation and Succession Planning

What policy does a company take to punish those employees who may engage in unethical and non-compliant behavior in order to meet company revenue targets? Conversely what rewards are handed out to those employees who integrate such ethical and compliant behavior into their individual work practices going forward? One of the very important functions of HR is assisting management in setting the criteria for employee bonuses and in the evaluation of employees for the bonuses. This is an equally important role in conveying the company message of adherence to a FCPA compliance and ethics policy. This requirement is codified in the Sentencing Guidelines with the following language, "*The organization's compliance and ethics program shall be promoted and enforced consistently throughout the organization through (A) appropriate incentives to perform in accordance with the compliance and ethics program; and (B) appropriate disciplinary measures for engaging in criminal conduct and for failing to take reasonable steps to prevent or detect criminal conduct.*"

Does a company have, as a component of its bonus compensation plan, a part dedicated to FCPA compliance and ethics? If so, how is this component measured and then administered? There is very little in the corporate world that an employee notices more than what goes into the calculation of their bonuses. HR can, and should, facilitate this process by setting expectations early in the year and then following through when annual bonuses are released. With the assistance of HR, such a bonus can send a powerful message to employees regarding the seriousness with which compliance is taken at the company. There is nothing like putting your money where your mouth is for people to stand up and take notice.

In addition to employee evaluation, HR can play a key role in assisting a company to identify early on in an employee's career the propensity for compliance and ethics by focusing on leadership behaviors in addition to simply business excellence. If a company has an employee who meets, or exceeds, all his sales targets, but does so in a manner which is opposite to the company's stated FCPA compliance and ethics values, other employees will watch and see how that employee is treated. Is that employee rewarded with a large bonus? Is that employee promoted or are the employee's violations of the company's compliance and ethics policies swept under the carpet? If the employee is rewarded, both monetarily and through promotions, or in any way not sanctioned for unethical or non-compliant behavior, it will be noticed and other employees will act accordingly. One of the functions of HR is to help ensure consistent application of company values throughout the organization, including those identified as 'rising stars'. An important role of HR in any organization is to help in building trust throughout the company and recognizing the benefits which result from that trust.

Hotlines and Investigations

One of the requirements under the Sentencing Guidelines is that a company "*...have and publicize a system, which may include mechanisms that allow for anonymity or confidentiality, whereby the organization's employees and agents may report or seek guidance regarding potential or actual criminal conduct without fear of retaliation.*" This requirement is met by having a hotline. One of the traditional roles of HR in the US is to maintain a hotline for reporting of harassment claims, whether based on Equal Employment Opportunity Commission (EEOC) violations or other types of harassment. It is a natural extension of HR's traditional function to handle this role. HR can assist in formulating an initial response to a hotline report to claims that may be (1) unfounded, (2) require immediate action, or (3) require a consistent workflow towards resolution. In addition to this initial assessment function, HR can assist in understanding if a report incident is localized in nature or system and in providing a consistent application of response. Lastly, HR is tasked with not only reporting, but tracking such incidents, and this recordation of data is critical to maintain the integrity of a FCPA compliance and ethics program in a company.

Regarding investigations, HR can bring broad benefits to any FCPA compliance and ethics program through an efficient investigation process. It is recognized that a

Legal or Compliance Department may wish to take over and complete the investigation process. However, HR can bring a consistency in both the process and any discipline which is imposed. Such consistency reinforces the senior management's message of commitment by the company to FCPA compliance and ethics. Such a function by HR can lead to an understanding of emerging risks. Lastly, it may be that employees are more willing to speak up to HR and the building of trust can be utilized to assist in overall risk mitigation.

The Human Resources Department in any multi-national company has a significant role in not only managing the employee base but in assisting to set the correct expectations. Consistent applications of these core beliefs and values will assist any company in remaining compliant and driving home the message that the company takes FCPA compliance seriously.

The Role of Human Resources in FCPA Compliance - Part II

Posted May 14, 2010

In our most recent post, we discussed that one sign of a mature Foreign Corrupt Practices Act (FCPA) compliance and ethics program is the extent to which a company's Human Resources (HR) Department is involved in implementing a compliance solution. In the prior posting we discussed training, employee evaluation, succession planning, hotlines and investigations. In this post, we will discuss background screening, doing 'more with less' and, finally, what to do when the government comes calling.

Background Screening

A key role for HR in any company is the background screening of not only employees at the time of hire, but also of employees who may be promoted to senior leadership positions. HR is usually on the front lines of such activities, although it may be in conjunction with the Legal Department or Compliance Department. This requirement is discussed in the Federal Sentencing Guidelines for Organizations (FSGO) as follows *"The organization shall use reasonable efforts not to include within the substantial authority personnel of the organization any individual whom the organization knew, or should have known through the exercise of due diligence, has engaged in illegal activities or other conduct inconsistent with an effective compliance and ethics program."*

What type of background checks should HR utilize in the FCPA compliance and ethics arena? The consensus seems to be that HR should perform at least routine civil, criminal and credit background checks. Care should be noted in any such request made in countries outside the United States as such information may be protected by privacy laws or where the quality of such information is different in substance from that of the United States. For instance in the United Kingdom, the request of a credit check can negatively impact a prospective employee's credit score so such a background check may not provide useful information to a prospective employer.

Additionally, although it may be difficult in the United States to do so, a thorough check of references should be made. I say that it may be difficult because many companies will only confirm that the employee worked at the company and will only give out the additional information of dates of employment. In this situation, it may be that a prospective employer should utilize a current employee to contact former associates at other companies to get a sense of the prospective employee's business ethics. However, it should be noted that such contacts should only be made after a thorough briefing by HR of the current employee who might be asked to perform such duty.

A company can also use HR to perform internal background checks on employees who may be targeted for promotions. These types of internal background checks can include a detailed review of employee performance; disciplinary actions, if any; internal and external achievements, while employed by the company and confirmation of both ethics and compliance training and that the employee has completed the required annual compliance certification. A key internal function where HR can be an important lead is to emphasize that an employee, who has been investigated but cleared of any alleged ethics and compliance violations, should not be penalized.

When the Government comes Calling

While it is true that a company's Legal and/or Compliance Department will lead the response to a government investigation, HR can fulfill an important support role due to the fact that HR should maintain, as part of its routine function, a hard copy of many of the records which may need to be produced in such an investigation. This would include all pre-employment screening documents, including background investigations, all post-employment documents, including any additional screening documents, compliance training and testing thereon and annual compliance certifications. HR can be critical in identifying and tracking down former employees. HR will work with Legal and/or Compliance to establish protocols for the conduct of investigations and who should be involved.

Lastly, another role for HR can be in the establishment and management of (1) an Amnesty Program or (2) a Leniency Program for both current, and former, employees. Such programs were implemented by Siemens during its internal bribery and corruption investigation. The Amnesty Program allowed appropriate current, or former, employees, who fully cooperated and provided truthful information, to be relieved from the prospect of civil damage claims or termination. The Leniency Program allowed Siemens employees who had provided untrue information in the investigation to correct this information for certain specific discipline. Whichever of these programs or variations that are implemented, HR can perform a valuable support role to Legal and/or Compliance.

Doing More with Less

The roles listed for HR in this series are functions

that HR currently performs for almost any US company with international operations. By asking HR to expand their traditional function to include the FCPA compliance and ethics function, a US company can move towards a goal of a more complete compliance program, while not significantly increasing costs. Additionally, by asking HR to include these roles, it will drive home the message of compliance to all levels and functions within a company; from senior to middle management and to those on the shop floor. Just as safety is usually message Number 1, compliance can be message 1A. HR focuses on behaviors, and by asking this department to include a compliance and ethics message, such behavior will become a part of a company's DNA.

So You Want To Buy a Business: The Role of FCPA in International Acquisitions

Posted February 2, 2010

The recession has lessened and all that cash your Company has been hoarding for the rainy days of the Obama years is burning a hole in your Chief Executive Officer's (CEO) pocket. He has his powder dry and is ready to make a big bang by going on a buying spree, targeting overseas entities, to beat the competition in coming out of your industry's downturn. The Legal Department is told to put together an acquisition squad and to be ready to go at a moment's notice. The job assigned to you is to make sure that your acquisition does not run afoul of the Foreign Corrupt Practices Act (FCPA) and to prepare a list of FCPA based due diligence that the Law Department should focus on to perform on the "Target Company". What should be on your list? In the recent article, "*FCPA Due Diligence in Acquisitions*" Securities and Commodities Regulation, Vol. 43, No. 2, January 20, 2010, lawyers from Squire Sanders, thoroughly explored this topic, through a hypothetical case it was based upon a "real life scenario". Some of their suggestions included the following suggestions.

I. Who is the Owner of the Target Company?

An initial inquiry should be made into the ownership structure of the target company. If any portion of the entity is owned or held by a government or governmental entity then such an entity is covered under the FCPA as a "foreign governmental instrumentality". There are several factors to consider in making such a determination. Some of these factors include: percentage ownership of the target company; control exercised over the target company; and how are the employees of the target company described by their country's government.

II. Are Agents involved in the Transaction?

Many times a "consultant" will be used in facilitating the purchase of a target company in a country outside the United States. If there is a clear and articulated business case for the Agent to be involved in the transaction, there should be due diligence on the Agent. It should include some a review of the Agent's credentials, ownership structure and financial records going back 3 to 5 years. Lastly, it is also critical to know the reputation of the Agent in the country's business community. If the Agent passes all these reviews, you establish a business relationship with a strong written contract.

III. Does the Target Company want you to pay for Travel?

What if the target company desires your business to pay for a representative to come to the US to visit your facilities? Such a trip falls under the FCPA and its proscription of "offering or promising anything of value". However, there may be are legitimate business expenses which can be paid by the US purchasing company under the FCPA; the key is to evaluate each travel and entertainment request. Generally, coach class travel and hotel expenses such as room charges, business center and telephone charges related to business can be reimbursed. Personal room expenses such as minibar, Pay-for-Movies and spa fees at the hotel should not be reimbursed. Receipts should be provided for any charges and if possible, the third party service provider should be paid directly rather than reimbursement of the target company's representative. Entertainment and business dinners can be reimbursed if there is a legitimate business purpose but personal, including the family expenses of the target company's representative, cannot be reimbursed under the FCPA. Lastly, do not give a "per-diem" in cash.

IV. Did the Target Company make any "Red Flag" Payments?

In your company's financial due diligence of the target company, did any evidence of "Red Flag" payments turn up which warrant further investigation? If such "Red Flags" arise, the US purchasing company must not turn a blind eye. If there is reason to believe that payments of the target company may violate the FCPA, further investigation is mandated. The recent conviction of Frederick Bourke for engaging in "conscious indifference" in that he knew, *or should have known,* that bribery and corruption was involved in the proposed acquisition, demonstrates the power of the FCPA in the acquisition arena. Red Flag areas would include the discovery of payments for gifts, entertainment, use of agents, facilitation payments or other payments which could not be adequately accounted for are discovered.

V. Are the Books and Records Reasonable?

In addition to its anti-bribery provisions, the FCPA also requires that a company keep such books and records which reasonably reflect the transactions of the entity and that there are proper internal controls. A key in this area is if the target company has any payments which are labeled as "miscellaneous" or there are payments which cannot be reasonably described. Gifts, entertainment and business expenses need to be recorded and documented. Internal controls are required to show that the target company has its statements in accordance with some form of accepted accounting principles.

VI. What Happens Afterwards?

Your Company has completed all the above steps but your due diligence has turned up items which cannot be resolved before your Company's President wants to fire that dry powder. What can you do? In Opinion Procedure Release 08-02, the Department of Justice (DOJ) gave its opinion on the steps required by a US company contemplating such a transaction. This opinion held that if Halliburton, in purchasing a target company, satisfactorily completed a rigorous, DOJ-mandated 180-day FCPA and anti-corruption due diligence work plan after the closing, then the DOJ did not "presently intend" to take enforcement action against Halliburton for any disclosed unlawful pre-acquisition conduct by the target company within 180 days of the closing. Halliburton was not the successful bidder for the target company but the DOJ's flexibility and Halliburton's open dialogue with the DOJ indicates there will be increased involvement between companies and regulators during FCPA acquisition due diligence.

VII. The End

The potential liabilities for failing to engage in pre-acquisition FCPA due diligence can be severe. Just how severe can be demonstrated by the eLandia acquisition of Latin Node. The FCPA Blog reported that "eLandia also disclosed that its purchase price for Latin Node "was approximately $20.6 million". After the acquisition, eLandia discovered that Latin Node had engaged in bribery and corruption. eLandia investigated, albeit after the purchase, and self-reported the violations to the DOJ. eLandia was assessed a $2 million fine, shut down Latin Node as an operating business and wrote off the entire purchase. For those of you keeping score at home, that is several years of pre-acquisition due diligence, plus legal fees for the FCPA investigation added to the fine, purchase price, business shut down and full financial write-off.

So what's the moral of this story? You can keep your powder dry but you must engage in full FCPA due diligence in any acquisition or transaction before moving forward.

The FCPA and Mergers and Acquisitions

Posted December 6, 2010

In a webinar on December 2, 2010, Michael Volkov, partner in the law firm of Mayer Brown and Ryan Morgan, Sales and Alliance Director of World Compliance, discussed the implications of the Foreign Corrupt Practices Act (FCPA) to mergers and acquisition.

They advise that businesses which seek to minimize their FCPA liability risks should pay careful attention to the potential exposure created by merger and acquisition activity. This is due to the fact that unwary companies can "purchase" FCPA liabilities by failing to conduct appropriate due diligence of their intended transaction partner. On the other hand, companies alert to those risks have been able to avoid successor liability altogether or, more frequently, obtain assurance about the scope of potential FCPA liability before the transaction is complete. Indeed, successor liability may attach in a stock transfer or merger because the assets and liabilities of the target company generally transfer to the acquiring company after closing; or the liability may attach in an asset purchase depending on the extent of the purchase and whether the target business is continuing or if the purchase agreement specifies which assets and liabilities transfer.

There are several recent examples where companies, which acquired targets, sustained large FCPA fines for the FCPA violations the acquired companies had engaged in prior to the acquisition. These include the Alliance One matter resolved this past summer with a $4.2 million fine for pre-acquisition conduct and $10 million in profit disgorgement. There was also the $240 million fine levied against Saipem for conduct of an acquired subsidiary of ENI, Snamprogetti, where the conduct at issue occurred over 2 years prior to the acquisition. One of the strongest examples is that of eLandia International Inc., which acquired Latin Node Inc., in 2007. Thereafter, it discovered potential FCPA violations, which it self-reported to the DOJ. As reported in the FCPA Blog, in addition to a $2 million fine, eLandia also disclosed that its purchase price for Latin Node "was approximately $20.6 million in excess of the fair value of the net assets" mostly due to the cost of the FCPA investigation, the resulting fines and penalties to which it may be subject, the termination of Latin Node's senior management and the resultant loss of business. eLandia eventually wrote off the entire investment by placing Latin Node into bankruptcy and shuttering the acquisition.

Volkov advocated beginning with a risk based assessment to focus the required due diligence. Such an assessment would focus on several inquiries, these would include such areas as to what countries does the target company operate in and how they rank on Transparency International's Corruption Index, including the level of corruption in each country. An inquiry into the targets business is also critical, for example does the target company sell to foreign governments and does its business depend on licenses or other approvals from foreign governments? A thorough investigation should include whether relationships exist among target company personnel and government officials through family and friends, etc.

After this more general business risk assessment, the review should turn to the policies and procedures of the target company. Basic inquires such as does the target have a FCPA compliance policy and how well does it maintain compliance records are a good starting point. Does the company have a hotline and does it conduct FCPA training? A critical inquiry is the use of third parties as foreign business representatives. Lastly, is the target company or any of its competitors, suspected or under investigation for corruption and are there any other internal investigations ongoing which should be reviewed?

Volkov also noted that after the due diligence is completed, and if the transaction moves forward, the acquiring company should attempt to protect itself through the most robust contract provisions that it can obtain, these would include indemnification against possible FCPA violations, including both payment of all investigative costs and any assessed penalties. An acquiring company should also include reps and warranties that the entire target company uses for participation in transactions as permitted under local law; there is an absence of government owners in the company; and that the target company has made no corrupt payments to foreign officials. Lastly, there must be a report that all the books and records presented to the acquiring company for review were complete and accurate.

The clear trend in FCPA enforcement is an increased and aggressive level of enforcement activity under the both the DOJ and Securities and Exchange Commission (SEC). Businesses must be particularly heedful in engaging in the mergers and acquisitions process, whether acquiring other companies or being acquired. Due diligence in these situations is critical and must encompass the full range of FCPA compliance issues. This article has provided to you a starting point for your analysis.

UTStarcom and Gifts and Entertainment under the FCPA

Posted January 5, 2010

To close out the FCPA year, on December 31, 2009, the telecom equipment maker UTStarcom Inc., agreed to pay the US Justice Department $1.5 million in criminal fines and pay the Securities and Exchange Commission (SEC) an additional $1.5mm in penalties to resolve Foreign Corrupt Practices Act (FCPA) violations in China and Thailand. Other FCPA penalties were agreed to by the company.

As reported in the FCPA Blog and the FCPA Professor last week, UTStarcom is alleged to have engaged in conduct which violated the FCPA which included:

1. Arranging and paying for travel to popular tourist destinations in the United States, including Hawaii, Las Vegas and New York City, when such trips were recorded as training expenses at UTStarcom facilities. However, UTStarcom had no facilities in these areas. These trips included a cash allowance of between $800 and $3,000 per person.
2. Spending nearly $7 million on lavish gifts and all-expenses paid executive training programs in the US for existing and potential foreign government customers from China and Thailand.
3. Presenting expensive gifts to, and engaging in

entertainment with, government agents, for example nearly $10,000 on French wine, as a gift to agents of a government customer and spending $13,000 on entertainment expenses for the same customer in an attempt to secure business.

4. Providing foreign government customers or their family members with work visas and purportedly hiring them to work for UTStarcom in the US, when in reality they did no work for UTStarcom.
5. UTStarcom was also alleged to have made payments to sham consultants in China and Mongolia while knowing that they would pay bribes to foreign government officials.

Guidelines for Gifts and Entertainment under the FCPA

The UTStarcom matter provides an opportunity to review the application of the FCPA regarding gifts and business entertainment expenditures to foreign officials. While gift and business entertainment is an area open to vagueness under the FCPA, as there are no clear guidelines in the FCPA itself or the legislative history, the conduct of UTStarcom goes far beyond anything that has been previously approved or discussed in any DOJ Opinion Releases. While prohibiting payment of any money or thing of value to foreign officials to obtain or retain business, the FCPA arguably permits incurring certain expenses on behalf of these same officials. Under the FCPA, the following affirmative defense regarding the payment of expenses exists:

> [it] shall be an affirmative defense [that] the payment, gift, offer or promise of anything of value that was made, was a reasonable and bona fide expenditure, such as travel and lodging expenses, incurred by or on behalf

> of a foreign official, party, party official, or candidate and was directly related to...the promotion, demonstration, or explanation of products or services; or...the execution or performance of a contract with a foreign government or agency thereof. *15 U.S.C. § 78dd-1(c)(2)(A)-(B)*.

There is no *de minimis* provision. The presentation of a gift or business entertainment expense can constitute a violation of the FCPA if this is coupled with the corrupt intent to obtain or retain business. With the above in mind, and the DOJ Opinion Releases, the following are suggested guidelines for gifts and business entertainment.

A. Gifts to Governmental Officials

Based upon the FCPA language and relevant Opinion Releases (Opinions 81-01, 81-02 and 82-01), a Company can provide gifts up to an amount of value of $250. Below are the guidelines which the Opinion Releases would suggest that a Compliance Policy incorporate regarding gifts:

- The gift should be provided as a token of esteem, courtesy or in return for hospitality.
- The gift should be of nominal value but in no case greater than $250.
- No gifts in cash.
- The gift shall be permitted under both local law and the guidelines of the employer/governmental agency.
- The gift should be a value which is customary for country involved and appropriate for the occasion.
- The gift should be for official use rather than personal use.
- The gift should showcase the company's products or contain the company logo.

- The gift should be presented openly with complete transparency.
- The expense for the gift should be correctly recorded on the company's books and records.

B. Business Entertainment of Governmental Officials

Based upon the FCPA language (there are no Opinion Releases on this point), there appears to be a threshold that a Company can establish a value for business entertainment of up to the amount of $250. However, this must be tempered with clear guidelines incorporated into the business expenditure component of a Compliance Policy, which should include the following:

- A reasonable balance must exist for bona fide business entertainment during an official business trip.
- All business entertainment expenses must be reasonable.
- The business entertainment expenses must be permitted under (1) local law and (2) customer guidelines.
- The business entertainment expense must be commensurate with local custom and practice.
- The business entertainment expense must avoid the appearance of impropriety.
- The business entertainment expense must be supported by appropriate documentation and properly recorded on the company's book and records.

C. Travel and Lodging for Governmental Officials

A Company should be able to bring foreign officials into the United States for legitimate business purposes. Once again, a key component is that guidelines must be clearly articulated in a Compliance Policy. Based upon Opinion Releases 07-01 and 07-02, the following should be incorporated into a Compliance Policy regarding travel and lodging:

- Any reimbursement for air fare will be for economy class.
- Do not select the particular officials who will travel. That decision should be made solely by the foreign government.
- Only host the designated officials and not their spouses or family members.
- Pay all costs directly to the service providers; in the event that an expense requires reimbursement, you may do so, up to a modest daily minimum (e.g., $35), upon presentation of a written receipt.
- Any souvenirs you provide the visiting officials should reflect its business and/or logo and would be of nominal value, e.g., shirts or tote bags.
- Apart from the expenses identified above, do not compensate the foreign government or the officials for their visit, do not fund, organize, or host any other entertainment, side trips, or leisure activities for the officials, or provide the officials with any stipend or spending money.
- The training costs and expenses will be only those necessary and reasonable to educate the visiting officials about the operation of your company.

The incorporation of these concepts into a Company's Compliance Policy is a good first step towards preventing any FCPA violations from arising, but it must be emphasized that they are only a first step. These guidelines must be coupled with active training of all personnel, not only on a Company's Compliance Policy, but also on the corporate and individual consequences that may arise if the FCPA is violated regarding gifts and entertainment. Lastly, it is imperative that all such gifts and entertainment be properly recorded, as required by the books and records component of the FCPA. One of the FCPA violations alleged against UTStarcom was that it falsely recorded these trips as 'training' expenses, while the true purpose for providing these trips was to obtain and retain lucrative telecommunications contracts. All business gifts, entertainment and expenses must be properly recorded.

Promotional Expenses Defense under the FCPA

Posted August 26, 2010

I. The Problem

So what is the problem with a US company paying for travel, room and board for foreign governmental officials to travel to the United States? The problem is that payment for such travel, lodging and expenses may run afoul of the prohibition against corrupt payments (or promises of them) made to obtain or retain business. The Foreign Corrupt Practices Act (FCPA) allows payments to foreign officials for expenses related directly to "the promotion, demonstration, or explanation of products or services" that are "reasonable and bona fide" 15 U.S.C. §§ 78dd-1(c)(2)(A) and 78dd-2(c)(2)(A). This affirmative defense, however, is notoriously hard to use (and easy to abuse), mainly because no one is quite sure what reasonable and *bona fide* really mean.

In his recent post on the FCPA Blog, UCLA student Kyle Sheahen, explored this issue in his discussion of his upcoming publication, entitled "*I'm Not Going to Disneyland: Illusory Affirmative Defenses Under the Foreign Corrupt Practices Act*". In his paper, he sets forth his proposition that FCPA enforcement actions provide "uneven indicators or what conduct the government considers covered by the defense. Consequently, in the absence of authoritative judicial interpretation or clear regulatory guidance, corporate managers are required to make educated guesses as to whether contemplated payments will qualify as "bona fide" promotional expenses."; he cites the following cases:

Promotional Expense Enforcement Box Score *(as of August 2010)*

Company	Trip Locations	Trip Costs & Perks	Company Facilities Present
Lucent Technologies	Disney World, Hawaii, Las Vegas, Grand Canyon, Niagara Falls, Universal Studios, New York City	$10 million in trips for 1000 Chinese governmental officials, including $34,000 for five days of sightseeing	None of the travel destinations
Ingersoll-Rand	Trip to Florence after trip to company facility in Vignate, Italy	$1000 'pocket money' per attendee	Facilities in Vignate but not in Florence
Metcaf & Eddy	First trip: Boston, Washington, DC, Chicago and Orlando. Second trip: Paris, Boston and San Diego.	First Class Travel and trip expenses for Egyptian governmental official and his family. Cash payments prior to trips of 150% of estimated daily expenses.	Wakefield Mass not in Washington, DC, Chicago, Paris or Disney World (Orlando)
Titan Corporation		Reference in company books and records of $20,000 for promotional travel expenses. Not clear if ever funded (Remember a promise to pay = making a payment under the FCPA)	

Not cited in Sheahen Paper			
UTStarcom	Hawaii, Las Vegas and New York City	Up to $7 million on gifts and all expenses paid trips to US	None of the travel destinations

While the Department of Justice (DOJ) and/or the Securities and Exchange Commission (SEC) brought enforcement actions against the above companies, this author believes that the facts of each enforcement action demonstrate that the expenses incurred by the companies were neither reasonable nor *bona fide* as required under the FCPA. These cases do not require a FCPA compliance professional to guess, educated or otherwise, as to whether the travel, lodging and expense payments listed above violated the FCPA. The payment amounts, as noted above, are so beyond the pale of reasonableness to be *prima facie* evidence of corrupt intent. Of course, it really does not help your case with the DOJ if you do not have company facilities in Disney World.

II. Opinion Releases

In addition to detailing the above enforcement actions, Mr. Sheahen also discusses guidance that may be gleaned from DOJ Opinion Releases on the Promotional Expenses defense. Here he points to substantive guidance for the FCPA practitioner. In 2007, the DOJ issued two FCPA Opinion Releases which offered guidance to companies considering whether to and, if so how to, incur travel, lodging and expenses for government officials. In Opinion Release 07-01, the Requestor Company desired to cover the domestic expenses for a trip to the United States by a six-person delegation of the government of an Asian country for an educational and promotional tour of one of the requestor's US operations sites.

Opinion Release 07-01 laid out the specific

representations made to the DOJ which led to the DOJ approving the travel to the US by the foreign governmental officials. These facts can provide good guidance to any company which seeks to bring such officials to the US for a legitimate business purpose. In Opinion Release 07-01, the representations made to the DOJ were as follows:

- A legal opinion from an established US law firm, with offices in the foreign country, stating that the payment of expenses by the US Company for the travel of the foreign governmental representatives did not violate the laws of the country involved;
- The US Company did not select the foreign governmental officials who would come to the US for the training program.
- The delegates who came to the US did not have direct authority over the decisions relating to the US Company's products or services.
- The US Company would not pay the expenses of anyone other than the selected official.
- The officials would not receive any entertainment, other than room and board from the US Company.
- All expenses incurred by the US Company would be accurately reflected in this Company's books and records.

For these representations, the DOJ noted, "Based upon all of the facts and circumstances, as represented by the requestor, the Department does not presently intend to take any enforcement action with respect to the proposal described in this request. This is because, based on the requestor's representations, consistent with the FCPA's promotional expenses affirmative defense, the expenses contemplated are reasonable under the circumstances and directly relate to "the promotion, demonstration, or explanation of [the requestor's] products or services."

In Opinion Release 07-02 the Requestor Company

desired to pay certain domestic expenses for a trip within the United States by approximately six junior to mid-level officials of a foreign government for an educational program at the Requestor's US headquarters prior to the delegates attendance at an annual six-week long internship program for foreign insurance regulators sponsored by the National Association of Insurance Commissioners (NAIC).

In Opinion Release 07-02 the representations made to the DOJ were as follows:

- The US Company would not pay the travel expenses or fees for participation in the NAIC program.
- The US Company had no "non-routine" business in front of the foreign governmental agency.
- The routine business it did have before the foreign governmental agency was guided by administrative rules with identified standards.
- The US Company would not select the delegates for the training program.
- The US Company would only host the delegates and not their families.
- The US Company would pay all costs incurred directly to the US service providers and only a modest daily minimum to the foreign governmental officials based upon a properly presented receipt.
- Any souvenirs presented would be of modest value, with the US Company's logo.
- There would be one four-hour sightseeing trip in the city where the US Company is located.
- The total expenses of the trip are reasonable for such a trip and the training which would be provided at the home offices of the US Company.

As with Opinion Release 07-01, the DOJ ended this Opinion Release by stating, "Based upon all of the facts and circumstances, as represented by the Requestor, the Department does not presently intend to take any enforcement action with respect to the planned educational program and proposed payments described in this request. This is because, based on the Requestor's representations, consistent with the FCPA's promotional expenses affirmative defense, the expenses contemplated are reasonable under the circumstances and directly relate to "the promotion, demonstration, or explanation of [the Requestor's] products or services." 15 U.S.C. § 78dd-2(c)(2)(A).

III. Travel, Lodging and Expenses for Governmental Officials

What can one glean from these two Opinion Releases? In light of the facts it would seem that a US Company should be able to bring foreign officials into the United States for legitimate business purposes. A key component is that the guidelines are clearly articulated in a Compliance Policy. Based upon Releases Opinions 07-01 and 07-02, the following should be incorporated into a Compliance Policy regarding travel and lodging:

- Any reimbursement for air fare will be for economy class.
- Do not select the particular officials who will travel. That decision will be made solely by the foreign government.
- Only host the designated officials and not their spouses or family members.
- Pay all costs directly to the service providers; in the event that an expense requires reimbursement, you may do so, up to a modest daily minimum (e.g., $35), upon presentation of a written receipt.
- Any souvenirs you provide the visiting officials should reflect the business and/or logo and would be of nominal value, e.g., shirts or tote bags.

- Apart from the expenses identified above, do not compensate the foreign government or the officials for their visit, do not fund, organize, or host any other entertainment, side trips, or leisure activities for the officials, or provide the officials with any stipend or spending money.
- The training costs and expenses will be only those necessary and reasonable to educate the visiting officials about the operation of your company.

Incorporation of these concepts into a Compliance Policy is a good first step towards preventing any FCPA violations from arising, but it must be emphasized that they are only a first step. These guidelines must be coupled with active training of all personnel, not only on the Compliance Policy, but also on the corporate and individual consequences that may arise if the FCPA is violated regarding gifts and entertainment. Lastly, it is imperative that all such gifts and entertainment are properly recorded, as required by the books and records component of the FCPA. One of the FCPA violations alleged against UTStarcom was that it falsely recorded these trips as 'training' expenses, while the true purpose for providing these trips was to obtain and retain lucrative telecommunications contracts. All business gifts, entertainment and expenses must be properly recorded.

We commend Mr. Sheahen for his upcoming publication, in which he thoroughly discusses the "Local Law" defense under the FCPA in addition to the "Promotional Expenses" defense. His work will add to the discussion of these two affirmative defenses and assist companies in crafting their FCPA compliance program.

CHAPTER III

INVESTIGATIONS, ENFORECEMENT ACTIONS AND LEGAL ISSUES

What is the Cost of FCPA Compliance? Or what is the cost of non-compliance?

Posted May 10, 2010

How do you measure the cost of poor performance? In the baseball world how do you measure the cost of the Houston Astros abysmal April and equally poor start to May, which is projected to lead to a 50-108 season record? One measure is the number of people who pay to come out to the ballpark. As reported in the May 2nd edition of the Houston Chronicle, the Astros home attendance is down 2,640 which translates into a per game revenue loss of up to $660,000. That works out to a full season loss of revenue of up to $5,436,000. This, of course, assumes that the drop in attendance is based directly on poor performance and not on other factors such as the drop in disposable income due to the economy or some other factor. But is this the sole measure of the Astros loss?

In the Foreign Corrupt Practices Act (FCPA) world, there can be a more direct relationship of the costs to a violation or even an investigation. For instance, a former investigation into a Nigerian bribery case involving bribe payments of up to $132 million led to fines and disgorgement penalties of more than ***$1.2 billion***. These fines and penalties do *not* include any costs for investigations, legal or accounting fees, other professional fees or drop in stock value associated with an investigation.

All of this brings us to '*Ding Dong Avon Calling*' and

the bribery probe of its China operations. As reported by Aruna Viswanatha, in MainJustice, on April 30 and Ellen Byron, in the Wall Street Journal (WSJ), print edition, on May 1, Avon has reported its costs for the alleged scandal which has engulfed the company. The investigation has now expanded from China to four other (unidentified) business units. CEO Andrea Jung is reported as saying, in an April 30 conference call with investors, "No conclusions can be drawn at this time," regarding the investigations. However, what Avon did report is some of its FCPA investigative costs to date, anticipated FCPA investigative costs, loss of revenue in China and loss in first-quarter earnings.

The expenses, both anticipated and occurred to date, and their earnings loss box score is as follows (as of May 2010):

Investigate Cost, Revenue or Earnings Loss	
Investigative Cost (2009)	**$35 Million**
Investigative Cost (anticipated-2010)	**$95 Million**
Drop in Q1 Earnings	**$74.8 Million**
Loss in Revenue from China Operations	**$10 Million**
Total	**$214.8 Million**

While the amount of the alleged bribery, or other corruption, has not yet been reported, MainJustice reported that the investigation is looking into "travel, entertainment, and gift expenses". It is difficult to believe that the $$ value of the bribes are anywhere close to the above mentioned investigation cost, revenue or earnings loss. The WSJ reported that Avon will overhaul its approach to sales in China, moving towards a direct selling approach, over the next 18 months. This certainly sounds like Avon is moving away from agents and distributors, the bane of many other US companies doing business abroad.

The WSJ also reported that the Avon investigation has expanded into its business practices in countries "selected to represent" each of its overseas regions. With slightly less than three-quarters of Avon's overall company revenue coming from outside the US, it may well be that the Department of Justice (DOJ) will want a more comprehensive review of the company's business practices worldwide, rather than simply "selected" business practices in "selected" countries. If I were Avon, I know I would want to do so, if not for the DOJ, but for my company.

How do you measure the cost of FCPA compliance? Put another way, can your company afford not to be FCPA compliant? What will the costs be if there are allegations of bribery and corruption in your company? Will the investigative costs exceed $100 million as they may well do in Avon's case? Will your fine, penalty and any profit disgorgement exceed $550 million as happened with Halliburton or simply be in the $330-$340 million range as with its former Joint Venture partners from the Nigerian bribery case? If you agree to a Corporate Monitor what will that cost be? As reported by Chris Matthews, in MainJustice on March 18, 2010, US District Judge Ellen Segal Huvelle raised the following spectra regarding Corporate Monitors during the Innospec Inc., Deferred Prosecution Agreement (DPA) and guilty plea hearing:

> It's an outrage, that people get $50 million to be a monitor," Huvelle said during a hearing in Washington, D.C., to approve a guilty plea for Innospec Inc., an international specialty chemicals company with nearly 1,000 employees. "I'm not comfortable, frankly, signing off on something that becomes a vehicle for someone to make lots of money."

This could lead to an Avon Box Score of costs which could read (as of May 2010):

Cost	**Amount**
Pre-DPA Investigative Costs	***$95 million???***
Pre-DPA Revenue and Earnings Loss	***$84 million???***
Penalty and Profit Disgorgement	***$100 million???***
Monitor Cost	***$50 million???***
Total	***How Many Hundreds of $$$ Millions?***

So will the Astros lose 108 this year or is there something they can do about it? Equally important, what will be the cost to your company for FCPA (non)-compliance and are you willing to risk it…or are you willing to do something to prevent it?

Who Will Have the Better Season?

Posted April 19, 2010

The baseball season is upon us and the Houston Astros have opened with their worst start since 1983. At 3-9, things may be looking a bit bleak for the hometown heroes. However several sportswriters have pointed out that the 1983 team ended up with a winning record, at 85-77. Things may be looking equally as bleak for Hewlett-Packard (HP) right about now. Will HP, or the Astros for that matter, come out of this with a winning record? At this point, it is too early to tell but this posting will review some of the issues that have been reported on the HP/Russia bribery and corruption scandal in the past week.

Several of this commentator's colleagues have noted something along of the lines of "even the WSJ has reported on this scandal, so it must be bad". The April 15, 2010 edition of the Wall Street Journal (WSJ) reported that German and Russian authorities are investigating whether HP executives paid millions of dollars in bribes to win a contract in Russia. German prosecutors are looking into the possibility that HP executives paid about $10.9 million in bribes to win a $47.3 million contract. Under this scheme, the company sold computer equipment, through a German subsidiary, to the office of the prosecutor general of the Russian Federation. The April 16, 2010, edition of the WSJ reported that the US Securities and Exchange Commission (SEC) have joined in with the Russian and German investigations.

As reported in the WSJ German prosecutors were investigating into whether HP ***executives*** funneled the suspected bribes through a network of shell companies and accounts in places including Britain, Austria, Switzerland, the British Virgin Islands, Belize, New Zealand, Latvia and Lithuania, and the US states of Delaware and Wyoming (yes, you read that right-the great state of ***Wyoming***). The bribery was said to be led by a German HP subsidiary, called Hewlett-Packard International Sales Europe GmbH, which, after receiving the payment for the Russian contract, sent about $10.9 million in suspected bribes back to unidentified officials in Russia. The bribes were paid through three German agents, who submitted fake invoices for non-existent sales and then paid the money on as bribes to un-named Russian governmental officials. The contract for hardware, including notebook computers, workstations and servers, were to be used by the office of the prosecutor general of the Russian Federation. It would seem that attempting to bribe prosecutors is generally not a good practice.

Both the Astros and HP would seem to have several unanswered questions about themselves right about now. We shall present some of these questions and hope they may lead to greater discussion of where the two may be going over the rest of the 2010 season.

Why didn't HP self-report?

The April 15, 2010 WSJ article reported that by December 2009, German authorities traced funds to accounts in Delaware and Britain. In early 2010, German prosecutors filed a round of legal-assistance requests in Wyoming, New Zealand and the British Virgin Islands, hoping to trace the flow of funds to new sets of accounts. Further, HP knew of the German investigation by at least December 2009, when police in Germany and Switzerland presented search warrants detailing allegations against 10 suspects. The New York Times, in an article dated April 16, 2010, reported that three former HP employees were arrested back in December 2009 by German prosecutors. Although it was unclear from the WSJ article as to the time frame, HP had retained counsel to work with prosecutors in their investigation. Apparently, since the SEC only announced it had joined the German and Russian investigation last week, HP had not self-disclosed the investigation or its allegations to the US Department of Justice (DOJ) or SEC. All of this leads to the second question; which is...

Where were the SEC and DOJ?

On April 16, 2010, the FCPA Professor wondered in his blog if it was merely coincidence that a few weeks ago the US concluded a Foreign Corrupt Practices Act (FCPA) enforcement action against the Daimler Corporation, an unrelated German company, for bribery and corruption in Russia and now it is German and Russian authorities investigating a US company for such improper conduct in Russia. The Professor put forward the following query: is such an investigation "Tit for tat or merely a coincidence?" And much like Socrates, he answered his own question with the musing "likely the latter". The WSJ Law Blog noted in its entry of April 16, 2010, that it would be somewhat unusual for the DOJ or SEC to stand by and watch European regulators conduct a sizable bribery investigation of a high-profile US company; phrasing it as "It's like asking a child to stand still after a piñata's been smashed open". With all these investigations going on we next wondered about...

HP's Response

HP has not taken all of this bad publicity lying down. Although the WSJ reported that HP learned of the investigation back in December, 2009, the only public mention of this "investigation" was in its March 2010

SEC filing. This filing did not disclose any potential FCPA violation but it did mention that "in many foreign countries" illegal business practices are "common". Such actions, undertaken "in violation of our policies... could have a material adverse effect on our business and reputation". Finally, as also reported in the WSJ, a HP spokesperson said, "This is an investigation of alleged conduct that occurred almost seven years ago, ***largely*** by employees no longer with HP. We are cooperating fully with the German and Russian authorities and will continue to conduct our own internal investigation". Well, at least ***largely***, the (alleged) HP employees who engaged in ***alleged*** bribery and corruption are no longer employees. Since HP had deemed fit to keep at least some of the alleged bribers and corrupters on its payroll; what is the "Tone at the Top?"...

Where was Carly?

The Buzz, reported on April 18, 2010, that former HP Chief Executive Officer (CEO), Carly Fiorina who is one of three candidates seeking the GOP Senate nomination for the state of California, has sought to distance herself from the scandal, saying that she was unaware of the alleged crimes and that she has not been contacted as part of the probe. However, one of the other candidates, Assemblyman Chuck DeVore, noted the obvious, by stating that the alleged crimes took place during Fiorina's tenure as CEO of HP. This commentator, who does not live (or vote) in California, has wondered about the effect of the investigation on her candidacy? If pressed further, she might well admit to being *shocked, shocked* to find out that bribery and corruption had occurred under her watch.

As many of you may recall, it was HP who reportedly ordered its 155,000 channel operation partners to take an FCPA compliance training course last October. Interesting, HP required these channel operations partners to also pay for this training. Such training was required in a very short time frame or the channel operations partners risked losing their status with HP. Is it possible this effort by HP was because they knew that an investigation was ongoing regarding its FCPA compliance efforts? We anxiously await further clarification on that issue.

So who do you think will have the better season, the 3-9 Astros or HP?

RAE and Settlement of FCPA Violations in China

Posted December 13, 2010

As reported on Friday, December 10, 2010 in the FCPA Blog and by others, RAE Systems, Inc., (RAE) a California-based gas detection company settled Foreign Corrupt Practices Act (FCPA) charges on this date with the Department of Justice (DOJ) and Securities and Exchange Commission (SEC) for $2.9 million. The DOJ's letter to the RAE Chief Executive Officer (CEO) and its legal counsel, dated December 10, 2010, declined to prosecute the company and its subsidiaries for its admitted "knowing" of violations of the internal controls and books and records provisions of the FCPA. The DOJ entered into this Non-Prosecution Agreement (NPA) based upon four listed factors, which were detailed as follows: (1) timely and voluntary disclosure; (2) the company's thorough and "*real-time*" cooperation with the DOJ and SEC; (3) extensive remedial efforts undertaken by the company; and (4) RAE's commitment to periodic monitoring and submission of these monitoring reports to the DOJ. We will review this enforcement action and NPA in detail and will discuss the facts underlying the allegations and findings of bribery and corruption.

A. Background

I. The Joint Ventures and Violations

a. KLH

The DOJ Statement of Facts, attached to the NPA as Appendix A, reports that RAE sold its products into China primarily through "two second tier subsidiaries" which were organized as joint ventures with local Chinese entities. One of these joint ventures, RAE-KLH, Limited (KLH) was originally owned 64% by RAE. This interest in KLH was initially purchased by RAE in 2004. Later, in 2006, RAE increased its ownership interest to 96%. Prior to its initial purchase of a stake in KLH, RAE conducted due diligence on the Chinese entity. This report made what the DOJ called "***troubling findings***" by noting

> As the important clients are those related to the government, it is very important for the company to keep very good relationship [sic] with those government people. In normal practice, KLH will determine its internal product price, the salesmen can negotiate the price with the client based on that and can take away the difference between the internal product price and the final sales price as commission. It is the salesmen, not the company, who will decide the [sic] whether and how much amount of the commission they should give to the clients. The salesmen didn't get the commission in cash directly, but instead they get the cash by provide [sic] different acceptable invoices. These invoices will then be used as original supporting documents for accounting records. They are recorded as different expenses in the financial statements. To some extent, the financial statements have been distorted by these commissions [sic].
>
> With the change of market regulations in

> China, the government influence will be less important, there is a challenge as to whether KLH could still keep these clients. Although KLH let the salesmen to deal with the kickback, still they are the employees of the company and they represent the company in the transaction.

Nevertheless, internal RAE documents simply noted that RAE knew "how much [FCPA] risk we are taking."

All of these practices were continued after RAE obtained its ownership interest in KLH. Indeed a RAE employee who reviewed KLH after the joint venture became effective noted "If you want them to be aggressive and grow business per set goals, they will do". This same RAE employee, commenting on the institution of a FCPA compliance program for the joint venture, stated:

> It will be a challenge to restructure because it changes the way they have been "successful" and rewarded in the past. As you know, KLH sales guy [sic] behave/get compensated as distributors and get "discretionary discount structure" (any residual = compensation to keep or to dispense as they see fit to close deal.) To kill the sales model that has worked for them all these years is to kill the JV deal value or hurt sales momentum.
>
> So we need to tread carefully in designing something halfway that won't choke the sales engine and cause a distraction for the sales guys. We knew this risk all along and have accepted it upon entering the JV deal.

After these reports, RAE did provide FCPA training and did inform KLH employees not to pay bribes. However, RAE seemed to believe that "we told them about [about the FCPA]...and that's all we can do." As you might guess, based upon this non-action, these bribery practices continued unabated even after such conduct was reported again to RAE management. The DOJ noted that while RAE senior management did indicate such bribery payment should cease, the company made "no effective effort to actually stop the practice." Most interestingly, the RAE Financial Controller in China was directed to perform an internal audit on these issues but "he never provided any findings."

So just what is "*troubling*" about this sales method? Initially, it appears that the sales person involved in each transaction sets the price, without corporate oversight. But for FCPA purposes the most troubling aspect is that the sales person involved would receive the difference in the internal product price and final sales price as a commission. To compound the problem there was apparently a double accounting of these amounts in the books and records which distorted the company's financial statements. This structure allowed KLH employees to use this money "under table greasing to get deals regardless if profitable/ collectible or not, kosher or not, etc."

The DOJ reported that as late as 2008, sales representatives of KLH used monies from this commission scheme for improper purposes. These purposes included the "corrupt giving of gifts and paying for entertainment, as well as direct and indirect payment, to customers".

b. Fushun

In December, 2006, RAE purchased a 70% interest in another Chinese company named Fushun. RAE also operated Fushun as a joint venture but included Fushun's financial results in the consolidated financial statements that RAE filed with the SEC. For reasons not stated in the NPA, RAE did not conduct pre-acquisition due diligence on Fushun. However, sometime later, RAE obtained information that Fushun did engage in business practices improper under the FCPA and, thereafter, failed to implement an effective system of internal controls at the joint venture.

II. The Payment Scheme(s)

As noted above, the KLH sales force set pricing and was able to obtain the difference between the price book pricing and the as-purchased pricing. In addition to this source of cash, which could be used for bribery and corruption, both joint ventures had reimbursement schemes through which joint venture employees would submit alleged Chinese governmental tax documents which did not support the claimed reimbursement, yet RAE would pay out cash for reimbursement purposes. From such reimbursements, gifts were made to family members of Chinese governmental officials and two contracts for "consulting services", valued over $300,000, were used to funnel monies to Chinese governmental officials. The Fushun joint venture used this reimbursement scheme to provide gifts to officials of state owned enterprises which included "jade, fur coats, kitchen appliances, business suits and high-priced liquor."

From all of the above information, the DOJ was able to conclude that RAE knowingly failed to implement a system of effective internal accounting controls at both joint ventures which was sufficient to provide reasonable assurances that: (i) transactions were executed in accordance with management's general or specific authorization; (ii) transactions were recorded as necessary to (a) permit preparation of financial statements in conformity with generally accepted accounting principles or any other criteria applicable to such statements, and (b) maintain accountability for assets; (iii) access to assets were permitted only in accordance with management's general or specific authorization; and (iv) the recorded accountability for assets was compared with the existing assets at reasonable intervals, and appropriate action taken with respect to any differences.

B. The Compliance Program

The Corporate Compliance Program is found on Appendix B to the NPA. In addition to the FCPA compliance policies and procedures specific to RAE, this NPA provides to the FCPA compliance practitioner significant information on the most current DOJ thinking on what constitutes a *best practice* FCPA program. Hence, this information is a valuable tool by which companies can assess if they need to adopt new or modify their existing internal controls, policies, and procedures in order to ensure that their FCPA compliance program maintains: (a) a system of internal accounting controls designed to ensure that a Company makes and keeps fair and accurate books, records, and accounts; and (b) a rigorous anti-corruption compliance code, standards, and procedures designed to detect and deter violations of the FCPA and other applicable anti-corruption laws.

The Preamble to the RAE Corporate Compliance Program notes that these suggestions are the "minimum" which should be a part of a Company's existing internal accounting controls, which should be designed to ensure that RAE makes and keeps fair and accurate books, records and accounts and that RAE maintain "rigorous" anti-corruption policies, and procedures which should be designed to deter and detect violations of the FCPA "*and other applicable anti-corruption laws.*". The RAE Corporate Compliance Program had thirteen points which are:

1. **Code of Conduct.** RAE should develop and promulgate a clearly articulated and visible corporate policy against violations of the FCPA, including its anti-bribery, books and records, and internal

controls provisions, and other applicable foreign law counterparts (collectively, the "anti-corruption laws"), which policy should be memorialized in a written compliance code.

2. Tone at the Top. RAE will ensure that its senior management provides strong, explicit, and visible support and commitment to its corporate policy against violations of the anti-corruption laws and its compliance code.

3. Anti-Corruption Policies and Procedures. RAE should develop and promulgate compliance standards and procedures designed to reduce the prospect of violations of the anti-corruption laws and RAE's compliance code, and RAE should take appropriate measures to encourage and support the observance of ethics and compliance standards and procedures against foreign bribery by personnel at all levels. These anti-corruption standards and procedures shall apply to all directors, officers, and employees and, where necessary and appropriate, outside parties acting on behalf of RAE in a foreign jurisdiction, including, but not limited to, agents and intermediaries, consultants, representatives, distributors, teaming partners, contractors and suppliers, consortia and joint venture partners (collectively "agents and business partners"), to the extent that agents and business partners may be employed under RAE's corporate policy. RAE shall notify all employees that compliance with the standards and procedures is the duty of individuals at all levels of the company. Such standards and procedures shall include policies governing:

a. gifts;

b. hospitality, entertainment, and expenses;

c. customer travel;

d. political contributions;

e. charitable donations and sponsorships;

f. facilitation payments; and

g. solicitation and extortion.

4. Use of Risk Assessment. RAE should develop these compliance standards and procedures, including internal controls, ethics and compliance programs, on the basis of a risk assessment addressing the individual circumstances of RAE, in particular the foreign bribery risks facing RAE, including, but not limited to, its geographical organization, interactions with various types and levels of government officials, industrial sectors of operation, involvement in joint venture arrangements, importance of licenses and permits in the company's operations, degree of governmental oversight and inspection and volume and importance of goods and personnel clearing through customs and immigration.

5. Annual Review. RAE should review its anti-corruption compliance standards and procedures, including internal controls, ethics and compliance programs, no less than annually, and update them as appropriate, taking into account relevant developments in the field and evolving international and industry standards, and update and adapt them as necessary to ensure their continued effectiveness.

6. Sr. Management Oversight and Reporting. RAE should assign responsibility to one or more senior corporate executives of RAE for the implementation and oversight of RAE's anti-corruption policies, standards, and procedures. Such corporate official(s) shall have direct reporting obligations to RAE's Legal Counsel or Legal Director as well as RAE's independent monitoring bodies, including internal audit, the Board of Directors, or any appropriate committee of the Board of Directors, and shall have an adequate level of autonomy from management as well as sufficient resources and authority to maintain such autonomy.

7. Internal Controls. RAE should ensure that it has a system of financial and accounting procedures, including a system of internal controls, reasonably designed to ensure the maintenance of fair and accurate books, records and accounts to ensure that they cannot be used for the purpose of foreign bribery or concealing such bribery.

8. Training. RAE should implement mechanisms designed to ensure that its anti-corruption policies, standards and procedures are communicated effectively to all directors, officers, employees, and, where necessary and appropriate, agents and business partners. These mechanisms shall include: (a) periodic training for all directors and officers, and, where necessary and appropriate, employees, agents, and business partners; and (b) annual certifications by all such directors and officers, and, where necessary and appropriate, employees, agents, and business partners, certifying compliance with the training requirements.

9. Ongoing Advice and Guidance. RAE should establish or maintain an effective system for:

a. Providing guidance and advice to directors, officers, employees, and, where necessary and appropriate, agents and business partners, on complying with RAE's anti-corruption compliance policies, standards and procedures, including when they need advice on an urgent basis or in any foreign jurisdiction in which RAE operates;

b. Internal and, where possible, confidential

reporting by, and protection of, directors, officers, employees and, where necessary and appropriate, agents and business partners, not willing to violate professional standards or ethics under instructions or pressure from hierarchical superiors, as well as for directors, officers, employees and, where appropriate, agents and business partners, willing to report breaches of the law or professional standards or ethics concerning anticorruption occurring within the company, suspected criminal conduct, and/or violations of the compliance policies, standards and procedures regarding the anticorruption laws for directors, officers, employees and, where necessary and appropriate, agents and business partners; and

c. Responding to such requests and undertaking necessary and appropriate action in response to such reports.

10. Discipline. RAE should have appropriate disciplinary procedures to address, among other things, violations of the anti-corruption laws and RAE's anti-corruption compliance code, policies and procedures by the Company's directors, officers and employees. RAE should implement procedures to ensure that where misconduct is discovered, reasonable steps are taken to remedy the harm resulting from such misconduct, and to ensure that appropriate steps are taken to prevent further similar misconduct, including assessing the internal controls, ethics and compliance program and making modifications necessary to ensure the program is effective.

11. Use of Agents and Other Business Partners. To the extent that the use of agents and business partners is permitted at all by RAE, it should institute appropriate due diligence and compliance requirements pertaining to the retention and oversight of all agents and business partners, including:

a. Properly documented risk-based due diligence pertaining to the hiring and appropriate and regular oversight of agents and business partners;

b. Informing agents and business partners of RAE's commitment to abiding by laws on the prohibitions against foreign bribery, and of RAE's ethics and compliance standards and procedures and other measures for preventing and detecting such bribery; and

c. Seeking a reciprocal commitment from agents and business partners.

12. Contractual Compliance Terms and Conditions. RAE should include standard provisions in agreements, contracts and renewals, thereof, with all agents and business partners that are reasonably calculated to prevent violations of the anticorruption laws, which may, depending upon the circumstances, include: (a) anticorruption representations and undertakings relating to compliance with the anticorruption laws; (b) rights to conduct audits of the books and records of the agent or business partner to ensure compliance with the foregoing; and (c) rights to terminate an agent or business partner as a result of any breach of anti-corruption laws, and regulations or representations and undertakings related to such matters.

13. Ongoing Assessment. RAE should conduct periodic review and testing of its anticorruption compliance code, standards and procedures designed to evaluate and improve their effectiveness in preventing and detecting violations of anticorruption laws and RAE's anti-corruption code, standards and procedures, taking into account relevant developments in the field and evolving international and industry standards.

The information provided in this Corporate Compliance Program provides the FCPA compliance practitioner and any company assessing its FCPA compliance program with the DOJ's most current thinking on FCPA compliance *best practices*. A professional third party assessment of your company's FCPA compliance program, using this format as a guide, would be a very strong first step to put your company into the mainstream of FCPA compliance and hopefully prevent or quickly detect and then remedy any FCPA compliance issue which might arise. As demonstrated by the relatively minor fine and penalty assessed against RAE, the benefits can be significant.

C. Lessons Learned

The RAE Agreement, in conjunction with the Deferred Prosecution Agreements (DPA) and the NPA for Noble Corp., released in November 2010 regarding Panalpina and related settlements, provide excellent guidance for the FCPA Practitioner. Each Agreement sets forth a complete description of the DOJ's most current thoughts on what constitutes the most recent *best practices* of a FCPA compliance program and in addition to this general guidance, the RAE Agreement provides specific guidance on joint ventures. More than going through the motions of performing due diligence on a prospective joint venture partner, a company must remedy any deficiencies found in the process should the transaction go forward.

Yet, as significant as the information noted above may be, I believe that the most significant lessons are learned from the RAE NPA is what did ***not*** occur. Even though RAE failed to follow the 2004 FCPA compliance *best practices* when it failed to engage in due diligence on the Fushun joint venture acquisition and even though RAE failed to take effective remedial measures with the KHL joint venture after it became a corporate subsidiary and after RAE had ***actual knowledge*** of FCPA violations; RAE did not sustain a criminal charge against it. In its Letter Agreement to the NPA, the DOJ noted "*...non-prosecution agreement based, in part, on the following factors: (a) RAE Systems's timely, voluntary, and complete disclosure of the facts described in Appendix A; (b) RAE Systems's thorough, real-time cooperation with the Department and the U.S. Securities and Exchange Commission ("SEC"); (c) the extensive remedial efforts already undertaken and to be undertaken by RAE Systems; and (d) RAE Systems's commitment to submit periodic monitoring reports to the Department.*"

Representatives from both the DOJ and SEC have been preaching the virtues and tangible benefits of self-disclosure and thorough cooperation with their respective agencies in any FCPA investigation or enforcement action. This RAE matter would appear to provide specific evidence of the benefits of such corporate conduct. The NPA reports that RAE had ***actual knowledge*** of FCPA violations yet no criminal charges were filed. Further, no ongoing external Corporate Monitor was required. Clearly RAE engaged in actions during the pendency of the investigation which persuaded the DOJ not to bring criminal charges.

Any company facing a FCPA enforcement action should study this matter quite closely and, to the extent possible, determine the steps that RAE engaged in or performed. The RAE enforcement action together with the Noble enforcement action which resulted also in a NPA, were reached with no external Corporate Monitor. No criminal penalties and no External Monitor are important examples of the tangible benefits for working closely with the DOJ in any FCPA enforcement matter.

When You Do Know What You Don't (Want to) Know - Frederick Bourke and Conscious Avoidance

Posted November 9, 2009

The Legislative History of the Foreign Corrupt Practices Act (FCPA) makes clear that Congress intended that the so-called "head-in-the-sand" defense - also described as "conscious disregard", "willful blindness" or "deliberate ignorance" - should be covered so that company officials could not take refuge from the Act's prohibitions by their unwarranted obliviousness to any action (or inaction), language or other "signaling device" that should reasonably alert them of the "high probability" of an FCPA violation.

In his recently denied Motion for New Trial, Frederick Bourke argued, among other things, that the jury instructions were wrong in a number of ways, including the *mens rea* element, the local law defense, a good-faith defense, and his possible conviction based on negligent acts.

As reported in the FCPA Blog, the prosecutors at trial contended that Bourke had "stuck his head in the sand". Even if Bourke did not affirmatively know that bribes were being paid, he was aware of a high probability such action was occurring and he consciously and intentionally avoided confirming this fact. In the jury charge, the Court explained this "conscious avoidance" could be equated to actual knowledge under the FCPA.

In his post-trial motion, Bourke argued that the trial judge, US District Judge Shira Scheindlin, had erred simply because he had "not tried hard enough to learn the truth". However, the test was not Bourke's actual knowledge of the payment of bribes, but Bourke's efforts to avoid acquiring that actual knowledge. "The conscious avoidance doctrine provides that a defendant's knowledge of a fact required to prove the defendant's guilt may be found when the jury is persuaded that the defendant consciously avoided learning that fact while aware of high probability of its existence", she said, quoting United States v. Svoboda, 347 F.3d 471, 477 (2d Cir. 2003).

The trial judge went on to state "In addition, the FCPA explicitly permits a finding of knowledge on a conscious avoidance theory. It provides that '[w]hen knowledge of the existence of a particular circumstance is required for an offense, such knowledge is established if a person is aware of a high probability of the existence of such circumstance, unless the person actually believes that such circumstance does not exist.' 15 U.S.C. § 78dd-2(h)(3)(B). Because the defendant must be found to possess the same intent as that required for the substantive offense, the conscious avoidance instruction was particularly appropriate in this case".

The successful prosecution of Frederick Bourke is a significant expansion of theories of prosecution under the FCPA. While the Bourke case involved an individual and his investment in one transaction, the red-flags that were (or should have been) raised are similar to those which a US company doing business overseas must investigate and evaluate in any transaction. All transactions must be thoroughly investigated, evaluated and reviewed on an ongoing basis to try and ensure full FCPA compliance.

FCPA Sentencing Box Score

Posted January 28, 2010

I am an avid baseball fan and as a child, was taught how to keep score at professional baseball games by my Grandfather. This had two effects. The first was immediate; it kept me quiet at ballgames. The second is more long term; I continue to keep score at baseball games up to the present. So I appreciates it when I reads (or hears) the words, "For those of you scoring at home" as was stated by the FCPA Professor in his December 31, 2009 posting on the UTStarcom matter. Judging from his posts, it appears the FCPA Professor is also a baseball fan.

In his post of January 18, 2010, entitled "Four Awaiting Sentencing"; the FCPA Blog discussed four persons, currently scheduled to be sentenced in January for pleas or convictions of FCPA violations. Two of the individuals are former Willbros employees who have pled guilty and are awaiting sentencing, Jim Bob Brown and Jason Edward Steph. The remaining are defendants all convicted at trial during 2009; Frederick Bourke, William Jefferson and the husband and wife team of Gerald and Patricia Green. , The Greens were the third of three high profile FCPA trials which were concluded in 2009.

The convicted defendants from the first two trials, Frederick Bourke and William Jefferson have been sentenced and are out on bail during their respective appeals. As mentioned in its "Four Awaiting Sentencing", the FCPA Blog stated that "Under the federal guidelines, Gerald Green, 77, is facing between 20 and 25 years in prison; the government wants him sentenced to life in prison." While a 25 year sentence for a 77 year old man is tantamount to a life sentence, it is not clear how much weight the trial judge would give to the Prosecution's proposed life sentence.

As pitchers and catchers are scheduled to report to Spring Training in only 30 days, the FCPA Blog article and the FCPA Professor's comment inspired the author's baseball mind thinking about the FCPA sentencing box score for the two defendants in the other 2009 FCPA trials and how that might related to those upcoming in 2010.

FCPA Sentencing Box Score (as of January 2010)

Defendant	Sentencing Guidelines	Prosecution Recommended Sentence	Defense Recommended Sentence	Judge's Sentence
William Jefferson	324 to 405 mos. =27 to 33 yrs.	27 to 33 years	"less than 10 years"	13 years
Frederick Bourke	57 to 71 mos. =4.75 to 6 yrs.	10 years	Probation	A year and a day
Gerald Green	235 to 293 mos. =20 to 24.4 yrs.	Life in Prison	Not yet reported	Sentencing now set for March 4

In both the Bourke and Jefferson cases, the trial judge gave jail time considerably less than that suggested by the Sentencing Guidelines and that sought by the Prosecutors; albeit with longer sentences than requested by the defendant's attorneys. So what does all this mean? The author comes from a civil law background so has no experience as a prosecutor. Perhaps a blogger with the prosecutorial background can help to explain these (apparently) wide discrepancies and what that might mean for Gerald Green.

Miranda and the FCPA: Do You Have the Right to Remain Silent?

Posted October 8, 2010

In a recent posting, the FCPA Blog posed the question of whether a company employee was warned "that concealing information from company lawyers conducting an internal FCPA investigation could be a federal crime?" The FCPA Blog raised this question in the context of a company's internal investigation regarding an alleged violation of the Foreign Corrupt Practices Act (FCPA). Even if the company attorneys handling the investigation provided the now standard corporate attorney *Upjohn* warnings, how does a company attorney asking questions morph into a *de facto* federal agent during an internal company investigation regarding alleged FCPA violations and is the attorney thereby required to provide a *Miranda* warning to employees during a FCPA investigation?

In a recently released paper, entitled "*Navigating Potential Pitfalls in Conducting Internal Investigations: Upjohn Warnings, "Corporate Miranda" and Beyond*", Craig Margolis and Lindsey Vaala, of the law firm Vinson & Elkins, explored the pitfalls faced by counsel, both in-house and outside investigative, and corporations when an employee admits to wrong doing during an internal investigation, where such conduct is reported to the US Government and the employee is thereafter prosecuted criminally under a law, such as the FCPA. Margolis and

Vaala also reviewed the case law regarding the *Upjohn* warnings which should be given to employees during an internal FCPA investigation.

Employees who are subject to being interviewed or otherwise required to cooperate in an internal investigation may find themselves on the sharp horns of a dilemma requiring either (1) cooperating with the internal investigation or (2) losing their jobs for failure to cooperate by providing documents, testimony or other evidence. Many US businesses mandate full employee cooperation with internal investigations or those handled by outside counsel on behalf of a corporation. These requirements can exert a coercive force, "often inducing employees to act contrary to their personal legal interests in favor of candidly disclosing wrongdoing to corporate counsel." Moreover, such a corporate policy may permit a company to claim to the US government a spirit of cooperation in the hopes of avoiding prosecution in "addition to increasing the chances of learning meaningful information."

Where the US Government compels such testimony, through the mechanism of inducing a corporation to coerce its employees into cooperating with an internal investigation, by threatening job loss or other economic penalty, the in-house counsel's actions may raise the Fifth Amendment due process and voluntariness concerns because the underlying compulsion was brought on by a state actor, namely the US Government. Margolis and Vaala note that by utilizing corporate counsel and pressuring corporations to cooperate, the US Government is sometimes able to achieve indirectly what it would not be able to achieve on its own – inducing employees to waive their Fifth Amendment right against self-incrimination and minimizing the effectiveness of defense counsel's assistance.

So what are the pitfalls if private counsel compels such

testimony and it is used against an employee in a criminal proceeding under the FCPA? Margolis and Vaala point out that the investigative counsel, whether corporate or outside counsel, could face state bar disciplinary proceedings. A corporation could face disqualification of its counsel and the disqualified counsel's investigative results. For all of these reasons, we feel that the FCPA Blog summed it up best when it noted, "*the moment a company launches an internal investigation, its key employees -- whether they're scheduled for an interview or not -- should be warned about the "federal" consequences of destroying or hiding evidence. With up to 20 years in jail at stake, that seems like a small thing to do for the people in the company.*"

When a Rose is not a Rose but a FCPA Violation

Posted July 2, 2010

We recently wrote about gifts and entertainment under the Foreign Corrupt Practices Act (FCPA). This week the Securities and Exchange Commission (SEC) announced an enforcement action involving Veraz Networks, Inc. The enforcement action generally revolved around what one Veraz employee termed in an email as "the gift scheme". Initially we would note that here in the US it is never a good idea to label any plan of action as a "scheme" and then to put it in an email as such labeling will always draw someone's scrutiny. The gift scheme was made with the purpose to "improperly influence" foreign officials who were employees of Chinese and Vietnamese government-controlled telecommunications companies to award or continue to do business with Veraz.

Veraz, or its agents with the approval of Veraz, paid for the following amounts as gifts and entertainment:

1. ***$4,500*** for gifts to the officials of the Chinese telecom company.
2. An ***unreported amount*** for gifts and entertainment for the officials of the Vietnamese telecom company.
3. An unreported amount for ***flowers*** to the wife of the CEO of the Vietnamese telecom company.
4. Finally, Veraz failed to keep accurate books and

records of all of the above.

The penalty reportedly paid by Veraz was relatively small for current FCPA standards. The FCPA Blog reported that Veraz paid a penalty of only $300,000. The FCPA Professor noted in his posting that in its Form 10Q filing for the period ending March 31, 2010, Veraz reported that it had shelled out $3.0 million to investigate and handle the FCPA compliance issues. So once again, the costs to investigate a matter are much larger than the final penalty. However, Veraz may still consider itself well off as there has been no report that Veraz agreed to a Corporate Monitor or that a Department of Justice (DOJ) criminal action is in the offing.

This enforcement action provides some additional guidance for what types of gifts and entertainment can be provided without one running afoul of the FCPA as this area is open to vagueness, and there are no clear guidelines in either the FCPA or its legislative history. While prohibiting payment of any money, or thing of value, to foreign officials to obtain or retain business, the FCPA arguably permits incurring certain expenses on behalf of these same officials. There is no *de minimis* provision set forth in the statute.

The presentation of a gift or business entertainment expense can constitute a violation of the FCPA if this is coupled with the corrupt intent to obtain or retain business. Under the FCPA, the following affirmative defense regarding the payment of gifts exists:

> [it] shall be an affirmative defense [that] the payment, gift, offer or promise of anything of value that was made, was a *reasonable and bona fide* expenditure ... and was directly related to...the promotion, demonstration, or explanation of products or services; or...the execution or performance of a contract with

a foreign government or agency thereof. *15 U.S.C. § 78dd-1(c)(2)(A)-(B).*

However, the Veraz case does provide direct and clear guidance in one area which has not been previously explored. It appears that a company should absolutely refrain from giving flowers to the wife of a company's Chief Executive Officer (CEO). In other words, do not make the call to the florist and remember sometimes a rose is not just a rose especially when it comes to FCPA enforcement.

Robert Kennedy, the Travel Act and the FCPA

Posted January 11, 2010

What does Robert Kennedy have to do with the Foreign Corrupt Practices Act (FCPA) and how has a nearly 50 year old statute aimed at US based organized crime now impacted the FCPA? It turns out quite a bit and perhaps it will be quite a bit more in significantly widening the scope of the FCPA.

Robert Kennedy's contribution is that while US Attorney General, he urged Congress to enact the Travel Act in 1961 which was passed as part of the same series of bills as the Wire Act and was a component of his program to combat organized crime and racketeering. The Travel Act is aimed at prohibiting interstate travel or use of an interstate facility in aid of a racketeering or an unlawful business enterprise. It prohibits the use of communications and travel facilities to commit state or federal crimes, but until now was mostly known for its use in prosecutions for domestic crimes. Its impact to the FCPA is that the Travel Act applies to foreign as well as interstate commerce; it can also be used to prosecute those US companies and individuals which engage in bribery and corruption of foreign officials AND commercial bribery and corruption of private foreign citizens.

The Travel Act elements are: (1) use of a facility of foreign or interstate commerce (such as email, telephone, courier and personal travel); (2) with intent to promote, manage, establish, carry on, or distribute the proceeds of; (3) an activity that is a violation of ***state or federal bribery***, extortion or arson laws, or a violation of the federal gambling, narcotics, money-laundering or Racketeer Influenced and Corrupt Organizations Act (RICO) statutes. This means that, if in promoting or negotiating a private business deal in a foreign country, a sales agent in the United States or abroad offers and pays some substantial amount to his private foreign counterpart to influence his acceptance of the transaction, and such activity may be a violation of the state law where the agent is doing business, the Justice Department may conclude that a violation of the Travel Act has occurred. For instance, in the state of Texas there is no minimum limit under its Commercial Bribery statute (Section 32.43, TX. Penal Code), which bans simply the agreement to confer a benefit which would influence the conduct of the individual in question to make a decision in favor of the party conferring the benefit.

The Travel Act was most recently used when four executives of Control Components, Inc., ("CCI") were indicted on April 8, 2009, for alleged violations of the FCPA's anti-bribery provision and the Travel Act. According to the indictment, the defendants conspired to make hundreds of corrupt payments with the purpose of influencing the recipients to award contracts to CCI or skew technical specifications of competitive tenders in CCI's favor. The Travel Act came into play as the Department of Justice (DOJ) alleged the CCI employees violated or conspired to violate California's anti-bribery law (California Penal Code section 641.3), which bans corrupt payments anywhere of more than $1,000 between any two persons, *including private commercial parties*. In the indictments, the Travel Act charges relied on alleged violations of California's anti-corruption law.

On July 31, 2009, CCI itself pleaded guilty to substantive FCPA anti-bribery charges and to conspiring to violate both the FCPA and the Travel Act. CCI admitted that, between 2003 and 2007, its employees made more than 150 corrupt payments and paid bribes to officers and employees of foreign and domestic private companies in violation of the Travel Act. CCI agreed to pay a criminal fine of $18.2 million and to retain an independent compliance monitor for three years.

In the July 31, 2009 Press Release announcing CCI's guilty plea, the DOJ referenced the Company's private overseas bribery. It said:

> According to the information and plea agreement, from 1998 through 2007, CCI violated the FCPA and the Travel Act by making corrupt payments to numerous officers and employees of state-owned and privately-owned customers around the world, including in China, Korea, Malaysia and the United Arab Emirates, for the purpose of obtaining or retaining business for CCI. Specifically, from 2003 through 2007, CCI paid approximately $4.9 million in bribes, in violation of the FCPA, to officials of various foreign state-owned companies and approximately $1.95 million in bribes, in violation of the Travel Act, to officers and employees of foreign and domestic privately-owned companies.

The CCI matter was not the first case to use the Travel Act in conjunction with the FCPA. As reported in the FCPABlog, is the matter of *U.S. v. David H. Mead and Frerik Pluimers*, (Cr. 98-240-01) D.N.J., Trenton Div. 1998. In this case defendant Mead was convicted following a jury trial of conspiracy to violate the FCPA and the Travel Act (incorporating New Jersey's commercial bribery statute) and two counts each of substantive violations of the FCPA and the Travel Act. In its 2008 article entitled, "The Foreign Corrupt Practices Act: Walking the Fine Line of Compliance in China" the law firm of Jones, Day reported the case of *United States v. Young & Rubicam, Inc.*, 741 F.Supp. 334 (D.Conn. 1990), where a Company and individual defendants pled guilty to FCPA and Travel Act violations, and paid a $500,000 fine. In addition to the *Mead* and *Young and Rubicam* cases "A Lay Person's Guide to the FCPA", on the DOJ's website, specifically states that "other statutes such as the mail and wire fraud statutes, 18 U.S.C. § 1341, 1343, and the Travel Act, 18 U.S.C. § 1952, which provides for federal prosecution of violations of state commercial bribery statutes, may also apply..." to US companies doing business overseas.

What does this mean for US companies doing business overseas? The FCPA Professor and others have written extensively on the broadening of the definitions of who is a 'foreign official' and what is a 'state owned entity' under the FCPA. However, with the incorporation of the Travel Act into FCPA prosecutions, these broad definitions may be completely blurred away if all foreign private citizens can be brought in under the FCPA by application of the Travel Act. US companies doing business overseas, which have a distinction in their FCPA compliance policies between gifts for, and travel and entertainment, of employees of private companies, and employees of state owned entities or foreign officials should immediately rethink this distinction in approach. The new decade is upon us and the Kennedy-era statute of the Travel Act may become as relevant in overseas law enforcement in the 20-teens as it was in the domestic arena for the past 50 years.

Nigerian Bribery Box Score

Posted March 26, 2010

Opening Day of the Baseball season is fast approaching and perhaps it is time to give a baseball statistician's view to the Nigerian bribery case. Yesterday, The Guardian reported that a UK court ruled that UK citizen Jeffery Tesler should be extradited to the US to stand trial. District Judge Caroline Tubbs, sitting at Westminster magistrates' court in London, rejected Tesler's arguments to fight off the extradition attempt. Judge Tubbs found that American prosecutors had alleged the crimes had a "substantial connection" with the US. She said that the Americans had already convicted one of the companies in the consortium for its part in the decade-long bribery scheme and one of the key executives who organized the corrupt payments. The Guardian, furthermore, reported that Judge Tubbs also rejected Tesler's argument that it would be "unjust and oppressive" to send him to America as prosecutors had taken a long time to charge him. Tesler had argued that he would no longer be able to get a fair trial in the US. However, the judge rejected this argument, pointing out that he was responsible for part of this delay, as he had hired lawyers to block prosecutors obtaining evidence from Switzerland.

One individual, former KBR CEO Jack Stanley has pleaded guilty to violation of the Foreign Corrupt Practices Act (FCPA) in connection with the matter. He was sentenced to 7 years in prison and is subject to ongoing cooperation with authorities on this issue.

KBR admitted that a consortium of which it was a member paid Nigerian officials at least $132 million in bribes for engineering, procurement and construction contracts awarded between 1995 and 2004 to build liquefied natural gas facilities on Bonny Island, Nigeria. The consortium was named TSJK and consisted of subsidiaries of the following entities: KBR (then owned by Halliburton); Technip, French company; ENI, an Italian company; and JGC, a Japanese company.

Settlement (or Reserved For Settlement) Box Score (as of March 2010)

Entity	**Fine, Penalty and Disgorgement of Profits (in $ millions)**	**Amount Reserved for Resolution (app. in $ millions)**
Halliburton (KBR)	**$579**	
ENI		**$350**
Technip		**$330**
JGC		None reported
Total	**$579**	**$680**

So for those of you keeping score at home, there has been and could be fines, penalties and profit disgorgement of over ***$1.2 billion.*** This figure does not include the amount paid out by these corporations for attorneys' fees, forensic costs and other professional fees which can be only speculated as ***priceless.***

This amount will most probably be paid to the US government but not to the Nigerian government, the country which is alleged to be the focus of the bribery. The FCPABlog has posed the question that *"Some in Nigeria will no doubt ask why the penalty money should end up in the U.S. Treasury and not their country?"* One reason could be that there is no current Nigerian investigation into the matter. In February, MainJustice reported that the Nigerian Senate subcommittee tasked with conducting the inquiry into the bribery scandal announced it was shutting itself down, saying that under the US-Nigeria Mutual Legal Assistance treaty, it could not obtain records from American investigators relevant to the investigation. While it does seem odd to this commentator that Nigeria would end its investigation of so public a scandal, we would conclude that Nigeria must have its own reasons for doing so.

All of this and Opening Day is less than 10 days away. We can hardly wait.

Technip Settles - The Nigerian Bribery Box Score Update

Posted June 28, 2010

Today the Securities and Exchange Commission (SEC) and Department of Justice (DOJ) announced, in separate Press Releases, that they both has reached settlements with Technip S. A. (Technip) for multiple violations of the Foreign Corrupt Practices Act (FCPA) for its part in the Nigerian Bribery Scandal. The SEC also charged Technip with books and records and internal controls violations related to the bribery. Technip agreed to pay a fine to the SEC of $98MM and a separate penalty to the DOJ of $240MM.

Technip admitted that a consortium of which it was a member paid Nigerian officials up to $180MM in bribes for engineering, procurement and construction contracts awarded between 1995 and 2004 to build liquefied natural gas facilities on Bonny Island, Nigeria. The consortium was named TSJK and consisted of subsidiaries of the following entities: Technip; KBR (then owned by Halliburton); ENI, an Italian company; and JGC, a Japanese company.

Technip also agreed to a Deferred Prosecution Agreement (DPA) and the filing of a Criminal Information. Under the terms of the DPA, the DOJ agreed to defer prosecution of Technip for two years. Technip agreed, among other things, to retain an independent compliance monitor for a two-year period to review the design and implementation of Technip's compliance program and to cooperate with the DOJ in ongoing investigations. If Technip abides by the terms of the deferred prosecution agreement, the DOJ will dismiss the criminal information when the term of the agreement expires. The Technip leads to a monetary count of the following:

Settlement (or Reserved For Settlement) Box Score (as of June 2010)

Entity	Fine, Penalty and Disgorgement of Profits (in $ millions)	Amount Reserved for Resolution (app. in $ millions)
Halliburton +KBR	**$579**	
ENI		**$350**
Technip	**$338**	
JGC		None yet reported
Total	**$917**	**$350**

So for those of you keeping score at home, there has been and could be fines, penalties and profit disgorgement of over ***$1.2 billion.*** This figure does not include any costs for reduction of credit ratings, the payment of monitor fees, including monitor law firm fees and any forensic accounting fees during the pendency of the DPA. The costs listed above do not include the total cost paid by Technip for its internal company investigation into this matter. However based upon the reported fees to date paid by Halliburton, these investigation fees will surely be in the tens of millions of $$.

We are now anxiously awaiting the settlement of the FCPA cases against both ENI and JGC to determine if the Nigerian Bribery Case will yield the largest total fine for one long series of FCPA violation. All we can say is *more will be revealed.*

And Then There Was One - The Updated Box Score of FCPA Settlements from the Nigerian Bribery Scandal

Posted July 8, 2010

Yesterday, both the Department of Justice (DOJ) and the Securities and Exchange Commission (SEC) announced the agreement by the Dutch company, Snamprogetti Netherlands BV, (Snamprogetti) to pay a $240 million criminal penalty to the DOJ to resolve charges related to the Foreign Corrupt Practices Act (FCPA) for its participation in a decade-long scheme to bribe the Nigerian government. In addition to the DOJ resolution, Snamprogetti and ENI also reached a settlement of a related civil complaint filed by the SEC, which charged Snamprogetti with violating the FCPA's anti-bribery provisions, falsifying books and records and circumventing internal controls and charged ENI with violating the FCPA's books and records and internal controls provisions. As part of that settlement, Snamprogetti and ENI agreed jointly to pay $125 million in disgorgement of profits relating to those violations. Both the DOJ and the SEC resolutions were discussed in yesterday's FCPA Blog and today's posting by the FCPA Professor.

Snamprogetti and ENI both also agreed to enter into Deferred Prosecution Agreements (DPA) and the filing of Criminal Information against each. Under the terms of each DPA, the DOJ agreed to defer prosecution of Technip for two years. It is noteworthy that neither Snamprogetti nor ENI was required to agree to retain an independent compliance monitor. If both Snamprogetti and ENI abide by the terms of the DPAs, the DOJ will dismiss the criminal charges when the term of the agreements expires. The Snamprogetti and ENI resolution leads to an update to the monetary count for the resolution of the Nigerian Bribery Scandal of the following:

Settlement Box Score (as of July 8, 2010)

Entity	*Fine, Penalty and Disgorgement of Profits*
Halliburton + KBR	**$579 Million**
Snamprogetti & ENI	**$365 Million**
Technip	**$338 Million**
JGC	None yet reported
Total	**$1.28 Billion**

So for those of you keeping score at home, there have fines, penalties and profit disgorgement of over ***$1.28 billion.*** All of this for bribes paid on, by, or on behalf of the four-company joint venture named TSJK, which totaled up to $180MM. This joint venture won four contracts from the Nigeria government between 1995 and 2004 to build LNG facilities on Bonny Island. The contracts were worth more than $6 billion.

This total settlement figure does not include any potential costs going forward such as reduction of credit ratings, the payment of legal fees and any forensic accounting fees during the pendency of the DPAs. The costs listed above do not include the total cost paid by Snamprogetti and ENI for their internal company investigation into this matter. However, based upon the reported fees to date paid by Snamprogetti and ENI, these investigation fees will surely be in the tens of millions of $.

As pointed out by the FCPA Professor in his blog today, the ***$1.28 BN*** figure amount is quite a pretty penny for the US Treasury. He poses the question as to whether FCPA enforcement has become a "cash cow" for the US Treasury. Additionally for those of you keeping score at home, could this case break the all-time fine set by Siemens? All we know for certain at this time is '*and then there was one* - JGC'.

CHAPTER IV

SUMMING IT ALL UP

Top Ten FCPA Enforcement Actions in 2010

Posted December 22, 2010

2010 has been quite an interesting year for Foreign Corrupt Practices Act (FCPA). As the year is ending I wanted to put forth some of the more significant enforcement actions for the FCPA practitioner to provide lessons learned and perhaps some educational opportunities for all our clients. One of the more frequent criticisms of the Department of Justice (DOJ) regarding the FCPA is that there is very little case law guidance or interpretation. The FCPA Blog has opined that this has led to his ***Big Lesson*** which is:

> "I know there's practically no FCPA-related case law, no precedent to follow, no *stare decisis* to light the way. So the FCPA is pretty much what the enforcement agencies say it is. And that's what's so very different and difficult about it."

However, in reviewing the past year, there is a fair amount of information which can be gleaned from FCPA enforcement actions. Additionally, it appears that the DOJ is tacitly responding to this criticism in some of the recent detailed compliance programs set forth in the Deferred Prosecution Agreement (DPA) and Non-Prosecution Agreements (NPA) that have been released in the second half of the year. With all of this in mind we submit for your consideration our Top Ten FCPA Enforcement Actions for

2010.

1. Alliance One/Universal Corp. - As noted by the FCPA Professor both the DOJ and the Securities and Exchange Commission (SEC), for the first time, issued a consolidated press release and consolidated an enforcement action against two unrelated companies. The companies involved in the investigations were the US companies, Alliance One and Universal Corporation, both in the tobacco merchant business. Alliance One's liability was predicated on successor liability for the FCPA transgressions of an entity it purchased. Both companies made improper cash payments, gifts and bribes in Central Asia and the Far East. The companies signed NPA's and there were criminal pleas by individuals involved in the criminal activity. It is significant to note that both companies self-reported to the DOJ.

These two matters provide to companies in the midst of FCPA enforcement actions specific steps that should be implemented during the pendency of an investigation to present to the DOJ. Initially, it should be noted that full cooperation with the DOJ at all times during the investigation is absolutely mandatory. Thereafter, from the Alliance One matter, the focus was on accounting procedures and control of cash payments. From the Universal case, a key driver appears to be the due diligence on each pending international transaction, and subsequent full due diligence on each international business partner. Next is the management of any international business partner after due diligence is completed and a contract executed. Lastly, is the focus on the Chief Compliance Officer (CCO) position, emphasizing this new position throughout the organization and training, training and more training, on FCPA compliance.

2. Daimler - As noted by the FCPA Professor, the DOJ stated in its Press Release on this enforcement action that Daimler (and three of its subsidiaries) "brazenly offered bribes in exchange for business around the world" and that Daimler "saw foreign bribery as a way of doing business." However, despite such statements, the DOJ did not charge Daimler with violating the FCPA's anti-bribery provisions. By resolving the case via a DPA, Daimler will not have to plead guilty to anything. Indeed, the FCPA Professor termed this as "yet another bribery, yet no bribery case."

Additionally, this matter stands for the proposition that a company can receive credit for self-disclosure under the US Sentencing Guidelines even if it does not self-report a possible FCPA violation. The DOJ investigation was started by a whistleblower report to the DOJ but Daimler nevertheless received a two-point reduction in its culpability. The US Sentencing Guidelines set the range of monetary fine as between $116 million - $232 million. However, the ultimate DOJ fine was approximately $94 million. Daimler did not voluntarily disclose the conduct at issue; nevertheless, the DOJ gave Daimler greater sentencing credit allowed for under the guidelines. The DOJ stated, "indeed, because Daimler did not voluntarily disclose its conduct prior to the filing of the whistleblower lawsuit, it only receives a two-point reduction in its culpability. The FCPA Professor noted that the DOJ "respectfully submit[ed] that such reduction is incongruent with the level of cooperation and assistance provided by the company in the Department's investigation."

3. NATCO - This matter continues the strict liability of a parent for books and records violations of a subsidiary. This matter was handled by the SEC and only resulted in a civil penalty, rather than a DOJ criminal enforcement. The case was unique in that it (according to the SEC Complaint) involved the creation and acceptance of false documents while paying extorted immigration fines and obtaining immigration visas in the Republic of Kazakhstan. "NATCO's consolidated books and records did not accurately reflect these payments." So from this case, one should glean that if a company pays money that is an extortion payment, it must accurately report such payments on its books and records. Otherwise such payment violates the books and records component of the FCPA.

One other factor in this case is that NATCO received a $65,000 fine and agreed to a Cease and Desist Order. However, the costs of the company's internal investigation were reported to be $11 million, "causing Natco cash-flow problems." So even if the result is a relatively small fine and civil injunction, with no criminal prosecution, the monetary cost to a company can be quite high.

4. Nexus Technologies, Inc. - In what the FCPA Professor termed as a "first" the defendants in this matter mounted a defense which challenenged the DOJ's interpretation, that employees of state-owned or state-controlled enterprises are "foreign officials" under the FCPA. Unfortunately, the trial court judge dismissed the defendants' motion with no comment or legal analysis so it provided no guidance for the FCPA practitioner on what may or may not constitute a "governmental official" under the FCPA. The interpretation defaults to what the FCPA Blog noted is that the FCPA is what the enforcement agencies say it is.

However, not all was lost by the defendants in this matter as it also demonstrates the differences viewed by the Courts and DOJ regarding sentencing of FPCA defendants. The sentencing recommendations by the DOJ and sentences passed down by the Court were as follows:

Sentencing Box Score (as of December 2010)

Defendant	***DOJ Requested Sentence***	***Court Imposed Sentence***
Nam Nguyen	14 to 17 years	16 months
An Nguyen	7 to 9 years	9 months
Kim Nguyen	6 to 7 years	Probation
Joseph Lukats	3 to 4 years	Probation

5. Nigerian Bribery Case - The conclusion of enforcement actions against Technip ($338 million) and Snamprogetti and ENI ($365 million) bring the total fines and penalties paid by companies involved in this matter to approximately $1.28 ***billion*** to-date. Additionally, this month, one UK citizen, Wojciech Chodan, was extradited from the UK to the US and has now pled guilty to violation of the FCPA. He faces 10 years in prison and is scheduled to be sentenced in February, 2011. Another UK citizen, Jeffery Tesler, has appealed his UK extradition order.

In an interesting development, the country of Nigeria recently charged former Halliburton Chief Executive Officer (CEO) Dick Cheney regarding the bribery payments. Earlier this week the Nigerian government announced that the charges were dropped for payment of a report $250 million fine. However, yesterday, Halliburton announced that the fine paid for the dismissal of the charges was "only" $32 million, plus $2.5 million in legal fees. The Wall Street Journal reported that Snamprogetti said Monday it settled with the Nigerian Economic and Financial Crimes Commission (EFCC) to pay a $32.5 million fine.

6. Panalpina Settlements - In what the FCPA Blog termed a history making day "for the most companies to simultaneously settle FCPA-related violations", the worldwide logistics firm Panalpina and five of its oil-and-gas services customers resolved charges with the DOJ and SEC, and another customer settled with the SEC for a total fines and penalties of $236.5 million. The customers of Panalpina which settled were Shell Nigeria Exploration and Production Company Ltd., (SNEPCO), a Nigerian wholly-owned subsidiary of Royal Dutch Shell; Transocean, Inc.; Pride International Inc., and Pride Forasol S.A.S.; GlobalSantaFe [now owned by Transocean]; Tidewater, Inc., and Noble Corporation which did not receive a DPA but was granted a NPA.

However, more was announced yesterday than simply raw dollars. Each resolved enforcement action provided to the FCPA compliance practitioner significant information on the most current DOJ thinking on what constitutes a *best practice* FCPA program. Each of the DPA's released yesterday, included the same Attachment C entitled "Corporate Compliance Program". This same information was also attached to the Noble NPA as "Attachment B". Hence, this information is a valuable tool by which companies can assess if they need to adopt new or modify their existing internal controls, policies, and procedures in order to ensure that their FCPA compliance program maintains: (a) a system of internal accounting controls designed to ensure that a Company makes and keeps fair and accurate books, records, and accounts; and (b) a rigorous anti-corruption compliance code, standards, and procedures designed to detect and deter violations of the FCPA and other applicable anti-corruption laws. It is noted that in the Preamble to each Corporate Compliance Program that these suggestions are the "minimum" which should be a part of a Company's existing internal controls, policies, and procedures.

7. RAE Systems, Inc. - Lessons learned. Companies are fully liable for their joint ventures actions and that even with actual knowledge of FCPA violations, conduct during the DOJ investigation can result in a NPA. However, this liability need not lead to criminal sanctions as RAE received a letter of Non-Prosecution from the DOJ. The DOJ's letter to the RAE CEO and its legal counsel declined to prosecute the company and its subsidiaries for its admitted "knowing" of violations of the internal controls and books and records provisions of the FCPA. The DOJ entered into this NPA based upon four listed factors, which were detailed as follows: (1) timely and voluntary disclosure; (2) the company's thorough and "*real-time*" cooperation with the DOJ and SEC; (3) extensive remedial efforts undertaken by the company; and (4) RAE's commitment to periodic monitoring and submission of these monitoring reports to the DOJ.

Representatives from both the DOJ and SEC have been preaching the virtues and tangible benefits of self-disclosure and thorough cooperation with their respective agencies in any FCPA investigation or enforcement action. This RAE matter would appear to provide specific evidence of the benefits of such corporate conduct. The NPA reports that RAE had ***actual knowledge*** of FCPA violations yet no criminal charges were filed. Further, no ongoing external Corporate Monitor was required. Clearly RAE engaged in actions during the pendency of the investigation which persuaded the DOJ not to bring criminal charges.

Any company facing a FCPA enforcement action should study this matter quite closely and, to the extent possible, determine the steps that RAE engaged in or performed. The RAE enforcement action together with the Noble enforcement action which resulted also in a NPA, were reached with no external Corporate Monitor. No criminal penalties and no External Monitor are important examples of the tangible benefits for working closely with the DOJ in any FCPA enforcement matter.

8. Gerald and Patricia Green - Although this FCPA criminal enforcement action was tried by a jury in the summer of 2009, the two defendants, husband and wife Gerald and Patricia Green were not sentenced until the summer of 2010. The trial judge's sentence would appear to reflect the growing disparity between the sentences that the DOJ requests and those handed down by the courts. The DOJ had originally sought a sentence of 25 years for Gerald Green (later reduced to requesting 10 years) and a 10 year sentence for Patricia Green. US District Judge George Wu sentenced the couple to 6 months each.

While this sentence reduction may result in more personal freedom, Judge Wu granted the DOJ's request for asset forfeiture, which means simply, as noted by the FCPA Blog, "any assets derived from proceeds traceable to a violation of the FCPA, or a conspiracy to violate the FCPA, can be forfeited". Each of the Greens owes $1,049,465 under the forfeiture, plus their shares in their company, Artist Design Corp., and its pension plan. The amount owed is so great that the DOJ is attempting to seize the home residence of the Greens because the forfeiture penalty cannot be fully satisfied without the proceeds of the home sale. The DOJ has obtained such complete forfeiture of the couples' assets in as much as they have filed *in forma pauperis* appeals.

9. Haitian Telecom - While this case generated much discussion in the FCPA world, particularly regarding an idea derived from an article in the Wall Street Journal entitled "*Democrats and Haiti Telecom*" that enforcement of the FCPA in Haiti should be suspended in the aftermath of the devastating earthquake which hit the island earlier this year. This was based on the fact that US companies simply could not do business in Haiti without violating the FCPA so they simply refuse to do so. To entice US companies to assist in the rebuilding efforts, the DOJ should suspend enforcement of the FCPA for some limited period of time. This idea was not seized upon by the DOJ.

While this debate was interesting, this case makes the Top 10 list because of what happened to the foreign officials who accepted the bribes. The FCPA only applies to bribe givers and not bribe recipients, the charges brought against the foreign officials who accepted the bribers were not FCPA charges, but rather a money laundering conspiracy charge. As reported by the FCPA Professor, these money laundering charges led to a guilty plea by Robert Antoine, a former Director of International Relations of Haiti Teleco responsible for negotiating contracts with international telecommunications companies on behalf of Haiti Teleco. He was sentenced to four years in prison. In addition, Antoine was ordered to serve three years of supervised release following his prison term, ordered to pay $1,852,209 in restitution, and ordered to forfeit $1,580,771.

10. Innospec - Fine and Penalty waiver for inability to pay? In March 2010, Innospec agreed to pay $40.2m in combined DOJ/SEC/SFO (UK Serious Fraud Office) fines and penalties for violating the FCPA and other laws. However, as noted by the FCPA Professor, it could have been worse. The SEC release noted that Innospec, without admitting or denying the SEC's allegations, was ordered to pay $60,071,613 in disgorgement, but because of Innospec's "sworn Statement of Financial Condition" all but $11,200,000 of that disgorgement was waived. The release states that "[b]ased on its financial condition, Innospec offered to pay a reduced criminal fine of $14.1 million to the DOJ and a criminal fine of $12.7 million to the SFO. Innospec will pay $2.2 million to Office of Foreign Assets Control (OFAC) for unrelated conduct concerning allegations of violations of the Cuban Assets Control Regulations." As noted by the FCPA Professor, "Innospec got a pass on approximately $50 million."

Top FCPA Investigations of 2010

Posted December 28, 2010

While enforcement actions can provide details of the most current thinking by the Department of Justice (DOJ) and Securities and Exchange Commission (SEC) on Foreign Corrupt Practices Act (FCPA) compliance *best practices* the public information made available during these investigations can provide, to the FCPA, UK Bribery Act or other compliance professional, many opportunities for teaching points and lessons learned by others. So with the opportunity for many educational occasions in mind we present our favorite investigations of 2010.

1. Avon - What is the Cost of Non-Compliance?

As noted by the FCPA Professor, one of the significant pieces of information to come out of the Avon matter is the reported costs. As reported in the 2009 Annual Report the following costs have been incurred and are anticipated to be incurred in 2010:

Investigate Cost, Revenue or Earnings Loss	
Investigative Cost (2009)	**$35 Million**
Investigative Cost (anticipated-2010)	**$95 Million**
Drop in Q1 Earnings	**$74.8 Million**
Loss in Revenue from China Operations	**$10 Million**
Total	**$214.8 Million**

2. Gun Sting Case - Organized Crime Fighting Techniques Come to FCPA Enforcement

On January 18, 2010, on the floor of the largest annual national gun industry trade show in Las Vegas, 21 people from military and law-enforcement supply companies were arrested, with an additional defendant being later arrested in Miami. The breadth and scope was unprecedented. Assistant Attorney General for the Criminal Division of the US Department of Justice, Lanny Breuer, who led the arrest team, described the undercover operation as a "two-and-a-half-year operation". The arrests represented the largest single investigation and prosecution against individuals in the history of the DOJ's enforcement of the FCPA.

As explained in the indictments, one FBI special agent posed "as a representative of the Minister of Defense of a country in Africa (Country A), [later identified as Gabon] and another FBI special agent posed "as a procurement officer for Country A's Ministry of Defense who purportedly reported directly to the Minister of Defense". Undercover criminal enforcement techniques such as wire taps, video tapes of the defendants and a cooperating defendant were all used in the lengthy enforcement action. In a later indictment, and seemingly unrelated to the "Africa" part of this undercover sting operation, allegations were included that corrupt payments were made to the Republic of Georgia to induce its government to purchase arms.

3. HP - Questions, Questions and More Questions

How does one begin to discuss HP's compliance year? From FCPA to Mark Hurd's very public departure for (alleged) sexual harassment, to the recent announcement, reported in the Wall Street Journal (WSJ), that the SEC is investigating Hurd in 'a broad inquiry that includes an examination of a claim the former chief executive officer shared inside information." However, we will focus on the FCPA matter which involves the alleged payment of an approximately $10.9 bribe to obtain a $47.3 million computer hardware contract with the Moscow Prosecutor's Office.

In an April 15, 2010, WSJ article, Mr. Dieter Brunner, a bookkeeper who is a witness in the probe, said in an interview that he was surprised when, as a temporary employee of HP, he first saw an invoice from an agent in 2004. "It didn't make sense," because there was no apparent reason for HP to pay such big sums to accounts controlled by small-businesses such as ProSoft Krippner, Mr. Brunner said. Mr. Brunner then proceeded to say he processed the transactions anyway because he was the most junior employee handling the file, "I assumed the deal was OK, because senior officials also signed off on the paperwork".

Why didn't HP self-report?

The WSJ article reported that by December 2009, German authorities traced funds to accounts in Delaware and Britain. In early 2010, German prosecutors filed a round of legal-assistance requests in Wyoming, New Zealand and the British Virgin Islands, hoping to trace the flow of funds to new sets of accounts. Further, HP knew of the German investigation by at least December

2009, when police in Germany and Switzerland presented search warrants detailing allegations against 10 suspects. The New York Times, in an article dated April 16, 2010, reported that three former HP employees were arrested back in December 2009 by German prosecutors. Although it was unclear from the WSJ article as to the time frame, HP had retained counsel work with prosecutors in their investigation. Apparently, since the SEC only announced it had joined the German and Russian investigation last week, HP had not self-disclosed the investigation or its allegations to the DOJ or SEC.

Where were the SEC and DOJ?

On April 16, 2010, the FCPA Professor wondered in his blog if it was merely coincidence that a few weeks ago the US concluded a FCPA enforcement action against the Daimler Corporation, an unrelated German company, for bribery and corruption in Russia and now it is German and Russian authorities investigating a US company for such improper conduct in Russia. The Professor put forward the following query: is such an investigation "Tit for tat or merely a coincidence?" And much like Socrates, he answered his own question with the musing "likely the later". The WSJ LawBlog noted on April 16, 2010, that it would be somewhat unusual for the DOJ or SEC to stand by and watch European regulators conduct a sizable bribery investigation of a high-profile US company; phrasing it as "It's like asking a child to stand still after a piñata's been smashed open".

In September, the WSJ reported that the HP bribery probe has widened and HP, itself, has announced that investigators have "now expanded their investigations beyond that particular transaction." This original investigation pertained to an investigation of allegations that HP, through a German subsidiary, paid bribes to certain Russian officials to secure a contract to deliver hardware into Russia. The contract was estimated to be worth approximately $44.5 million and the alleged bribes paid were approximately $10.9 million. In a later 10-Q filing, HP stated that the investigation has now expanded into transactions "in Russia and in the Commonwealth of Independent States sub region dating back to 2000." The WSJ noted that US public companies, such as HP, are only required to report FCPA investigations in SEC filings if they "are material for investors."

4. Team Inc., - No *de minimis* Exception in FCPA

As reported by the FCPA Professor, in August 2009, Team Inc. disclosed that an internal investigation conducted by FCPA counsel "found evidence suggesting that payments, which may violate the Foreign Corrupt Practices Act (FCPA), were made to employees of foreign government owned enterprises." The release further noted that "[b]ased upon the evidence obtained to date, we believe that the total of these improper payments over the past five years did not exceed $50,000. The total annual revenues from the impacted Trinidad branch represent approximately one-half of one percent of our annual consolidated revenues. Team voluntary disclosed information relating to the initial allegations, the investigation and the initial findings to the U.S. Department of Justice and to the Securities and Exchange Commission, and we will cooperate with the DOJ and SEC in connection with their review of this matter."

There is no *de minim*is exception found in the FCPA there are books and records and internal control provisions applicable to issuers like Team. Thus, even if the payments were not material in terms of the company's overall financial condition, there still could be FCPA books and records and internal control exposure if they were misrecorded in the company's books and records or made in the absence of any internal controls.

In its 8K, filed on January 8, 2010, Team reported "As previously reported, the Audit Committee is conducting an independent investigation regarding possible violations of the Foreign Corrupt Practices Act ("FCPA") in cooperation with the U.S. Department of Justice and the Securities and Exchange Commission. While the investigation is ongoing, management continues to believe that any possible violations of the FCPA are limited in size and scope. The investigation is now expected to be completed during the first calendar quarter of 2010. The total professional costs associated with the investigation are now projected to be about $3.0 million."

So the FCPA Professor posed the question:

"*A $3 million dollar internal investigation concerning non-material payments made by a branch office that represents less than one-half of one percent of the company's annual consolidated revenues*?"

And his answer: ***"Wow!"***

In August, 2010, when disclosing its interim financial results for the year, Team reported, "The results of the FCPA investigation were communicated to the SEC and Department of Justice in May 2010 and the Company is awaiting their response. The results of the independent investigation support management's belief that any possible violations of the FCPA were limited in size and scope. The total professional costs associated with the investigation were approximately $3.2 million."

So $50,000 in (possibly) illegal payments equate to over $3 million investigative costs, so far.

5. ALSTOM - Arrests in the Board Room

As reported by the FCPA Blog, the UK Serious Fraud Office (SFO) reported in dramatic fashion the arrest of three top executives of French industrial giant ALSTOM's British unit. The three Alstom Board members were suspected of paying bribes overseas to win contracts.

The SFO Press Release stated that "[t]hree members of the Board of ALSTOM in the UK have been arrested on suspicion of bribery and corruption, conspiracy to pay bribes, money laundering and false accounting, and have been taken to police stations to be interviewed by the Serious Fraud Office."

According to the release, search warrants were executed at five Alstom business premises and four residential addresses. The operation, involving "109 SFO staff and 44 police officers", is code-named "Operation Ruthenium" and centers on "suspected payment of bribes by companies within the ALSTOM group in the U.K." According to the release, "[i]t is suspected that bribes have been paid in order to win contracts overseas."

Alstom released a statement which said:

Several Alstom offices in the United Kingdom have been raided on Wednesday 24 March by police officers and some of its local managers are being questioned. The police apparently executed search warrants upon the request of the Swiss Federal justice. Alstom has been investigated by the Swiss justice for more than 3 years on the motive of alleged bribery issues. Within this frame, Alstom's offices in Switzerland and France have already been searched in the past years. Alstom is cooperating with the British authorities.

6. PBS&J - The Effect of an Ongoing FCPA Investigation in a Merger and Acquisition

As reported by the FCPA Blog, in what may be the first case of its kind, a US company that has no securities traded on an exchange but files periodic reports with the SEC disclosed an internal investigation into possible FCPA violations. The matter involved PBS&J Corporation, which in January, 2010, stated that it would not satisfy the filing deadline for its Annual Report on Form 10-K for the year ended September 30, 2009 "due to an internal investigation being conducted by the Audit Committee of the Board of Directors." The company said the purpose of the internal investigation "is to determine whether any laws have been violated, including the Foreign Corrupt Practices Act, in connection with certain projects undertaken by PBS&J International, Inc., one of the Company's subsidiaries, in certain foreign countries."

However, this was not the reason that PBS&J made our Top 10 list. In the spring and summer of 2010, PBS&J sought bidders for itself. One of the concerns was the ongoing and unresolved FCPA investigation. PBS&J whittled the bidders down to two finalists, Company A and Company B. Company B had a higher bid price but demanded that the merger agreement include additional closing conditions regarding the FCPA investigation and a definition of "Company Material Adverse Effect" that would have allowed Company B to terminate the merger agreement in the event of adverse developments in the FCPA investigation. PSB&J declined to provide this in the closing documents and so PBS&J took a lower stock price for its shareholders because of its unresolved FCPA investigation.

7. Schlumberger - Red Flags, Red Flags and More Red Flags

In October, the WSJ reported that the DOJ was investigating allegations of possible bribery in Yemen by Schlumberger Ltd., (SLB) in connection with SLB's 2002 agreement with the Yemen government to create a national exploration data-bank for the country's oil industry. The allegations involve a foreign business representative, Zonic Invest Ltd., which became involved in the 2002 Data Bank Development Project between SLB and Yemen's national oil company, the Petroleum Exploration and Production Authority (PEPA). Zonic's General Director is the nephew of the then and current President of Yemen,

Ali Abdullah Saleh. From the WSJ article, it was not clear the precise business relationship between SLB and Zonic, for instance: whether Zonic was an agent of SLB, a joint venture partner or simply a contractor.

In the WSJ article there were several reported allegations which stand out as classic ***Red Flags*** in FCPA compliance policies. Initially, PEPA had urged SLB to hire Zonic as a go-between at, or near, the time the contractual negotiations were nearing conclusion. Second the data-bank project went forward after SLB "agreed to hire and pay Zonic a $500,000 signing bonus" then the contract between SLB and PEPA was concluded. Indeed, the General Director of Zonic was quoted as saying, "If it wasn't for Zonic, there would have been no data-bank project." Lastly, the WSJ article does not reference that any written contract was executed between SLB and Zonic for this $500,000 payment.

With as many ***Red Flags*** that may have been raised in the WSJ report of the actions and statements that transpired before the contract for the data-bank project was concluded between SLB and PEPA, there were several raised thereafter. After the contract was concluded, WSJ reported that internal SLB documents revealed that "Zonic wanted a roughly 20% cut of Schlumberger's profits from the project." While SLB did not agree to pay such percentage of profits outright, it was noted that SLB's documents stated that the Yemen country manager had "suggested that those amounts could be compensated [to Zonic] through services." These services were said to include providing personnel to the project, networking, furniture and computer hardware. Payments for such services were made, even though there was no contract between SLB and Zonic, from 2002 to 2004. A contractual relationship between the parties was established in 2004 and lasted until at least 2007. The total amount paid by SLB to Zonic was reported to be $1.38 from 2003 to

2007. However, with regards to the services and products supplied by Zonic to SLB, the WSJ noted that some were "above market rate" and others were unnecessary; specifically noting that over $200,000 was paid for certain computer hardware, "although Schlumberger itself was among the leading providers of such hardware." The Daily Finance Blog reported, on October 8, 2010, that Zonic did not provide some of the services for which it was paid.

8. CB Richard Ellis - No Business or Industry is Immune from the FCPA

In October, CB Richard Ellis (CBRE), global real estate firm disclosed possible FCPA violations related to its operations in China. As reported by the FCPA Blog, the Company detailed in a SEC filing that its employees made payments for entertainment and gifts to Chinese government officials, which were discovered during an internal investigation. The Company said in the filing that it has "As a result of an internal investigation that began in the first quarter of 2010, ...determined that some of its employees in certain of its offices in China made payments in violation of Company policy to local governmental officials, including payments for non–business entertainment and in the form of gifts." The payments CBRE discovered are minor in amount and believes relate to only a few discrete transactions involving immaterial revenues. CBRE also said that it had self-disclosed the payments to the DOJ and SEC in February, 2010. It has been cooperating with the agencies and has taken other unspecified "remedial measures."

As reported by the FCPA Professor, CBRE also reported a second investigation, which began in the third quarter of 2010. It was labeled as an "internal investigation, with the assistance of outside counsel, involving the use of a third party agent in connection with a purchase in 2008 of an investment property in China for one of the funds the Company manages through its Global Investment Management business. This investigation is ongoing and at this point the Company is unable to predict the duration, scope or results thereof. In light of the Company's cooperation with the DOJ and the SEC as described above, the Company voluntarily notified both agencies of this separate internal investigation and will report back to them when the Company has more information."

Most businesses believe that the DOJ and SEC target industries or sectors which work traditionally in countries where corruption is perceived to be endemic, such as the energy sector. However, this CBRE investigation clearly demonstrates that any company which does business overseas needs to have a full FCPA compliance program in place.

9. Dalian - Welcome to the (FCPA) Club

In what the FCPA Professor termed the first focus of a FCPA inquiry on a China-based issuer, the Chinese company Dalian disclosed in an SEC filing that it was notified that the SEC was "conducting a formal investigation relating to the Company's financial reporting and compliance with the Foreign Corrupt Practices Act for the period January 1, 2008 through the present. The Company is cooperating with the SEC's investigation. It is not possible to predict the outcome of the investigation, including whether or when any proceedings might be initiated, when these matters may be resolved or what if any penalties or other remedies may be imposed."

As reported in the WSJ, the DOJ and the SEC have never charged a listed Chinese company. At least two Chinese subsidiaries of US issuers, DaimlerChrysler China Ltd., now known as Daimler North East Asia Ltd., and DPC (Tianjin) Co. Ltd., a medical products company, have settled foreign bribery charges with the agencies. But now we have the first Chinese issuer. All we can say is to quote the FCPA Professor, "*Welcome to the Club*".

10. SciClone - Hell Hath no Fury like a SEC Subpoena

The pharmaceutical company SciClone had a fairly tumultuous August and September. It included the following:

August 10th - Shares of the Company as low as 40% down from the previous day's close, closing down 31.9%. Levi & Korsinsky, The Law Offices of Howard G. Smith LLP, the law firm of Kahn Swick & Foti, LLC, and the law firm of Roy Jacobs & Associates all announced that they were investigating SciClone on behalf of shareholders for possible violations of state and federal securities laws.

August 11th - The law firms of Pomerantz Haudek Grossman & Gross, Statman, Harris & Eyrich, Goldfarb Branham and Finkelstein Thompson all announced that they were investigating claims on behalf of investors of SciClone to determine whether it has violated federal securities laws.

August 12th - The law firm of Robbins Umeda announced that it commenced an investigation into possible breaches of fiduciary duty and other violations of the law by certain officers and directors at the Company.

August 13th - The law firm of Kahn Swick & Foti announced that the firm has filed the first securities fraud class action lawsuit against SciClone in the United States District Court for the Northern District of California.

August 19th - The law firms of Barroway Topaz Kessler Meltzer & Check and Brower Piven both announced that they had filed class action lawsuits in the United States District Court for the Northern District of California on behalf of purchasers of the securities of SciClone and purchasers of the common stock of SciClone.

August 20th - The law firm of Kendall Law Group announced an investigation of SciClone for shareholders.

Unfortunately, another class action law suit was filed, this time by the law firm of Ryan & Maniskas.

August 28th - The law firm of Roy Jacobs & Associates (again) announced that it was investigating SciClone for potentially violating the federal securities laws.

September 7th - The Shuman Law Firm announced that it had filed a class action lawsuit against the Company.

September 8th – The law firm of Kaplan Fox & Kilsheimer announced that it had filed a class action suit against SciClone.

September 16th - The law firm of Strauss & Troy announced that it had filed a class action lawsuit against SciClone for potential violations of state and federal law.

September 23rd - The law firm of Lieff Cabraser Heimann & Bernstein announce that class action lawsuits have been brought on behalf of purchasers of the common stock of SciClone.

So what did SciClone actually do? The FCPA Professor reported that on August 9th, SciClone announced that it had been contacted by the SEC and was advised that the SEC has initiated a formal, non-public investigation. In connection with this investigation, the SEC had issued a subpoena to SciClone requesting a variety of documents and other information. The subpoena requested documents relating to a range of matters including: interactions with regulators and government-owned entities in China, activities relating to sales in China and documents relating to certain company financial and other disclosures. On August 6, 2010, the Company received a letter from the DOJ indicating that the DOJ was investigating FCPA issues in the pharmaceutical industry generally, and had received information about the Company's practices suggesting possible violations.

During SciClone's August 9th earnings conference call, the Company President and Chief Executive Officer

Friedhelm Blobel stated that SciClone "intends to cooperate fully with the SEC and DOJ in the conduct of their investigations, and has appointed a special committee of independent directors to oversee the Company's efforts." Blobel noted that "as far as timing is concerned, the lawyers tell us that these investigations typically are long lasting." We would opine that his lawyers got that point "spot on".

Looking Back – Top FCPA Issues from 2010

Posted December 31, 2010

We conclude our blog this year with some of our favorite Foreign Corrupt Practices Act (FCPA) issues that have arisen or were discussed in 2010.

The following list is not exhaustive but is designed to supplement our prior posts on our top enforcement actions and investigations from 2010 with other issues we felt were of importance to the FCPA compliance and ethics practitioner.

I. Amendments to the FCPA

At what the FCPA Blog termed "an unprecedented investigation into the Department of Justice's (DOJ) enforcement of the Foreign Corrupt Practices Act (FCPA)", in a hearing on November 30, 2010, entitled the "*Examining Enforcement of the Foreign Corrupt Practices Act*", before the US Senate Judiciary Committee, Subcommittee on Crime and Drugs, three panelists Butler University Professor Michael Koehler, and attorneys Andrew Wiessmann, of Jenner and Block, and Michael Volkov, of Mayer Brown, presented proposed amendments to the FCPA.

Professor Michael Koehler (a/k/a The FCPA Professor)

Professor Koehler focused on two issues; (1) the lack of individual prosecutions; and (2) what he believes is an over-expansive definition of foreign governmental official. The DOJ's theory of prosecution was based on the claim that employees of alleged [state-owned enterprises] were "foreign officials" under the FCPA – an interpretation Professor Koehler believes is contrary to Congressional intent. Prosecuting individuals is a key to achieving deterrence in the FCPA context and should thus be a "cornerstone" of the DOJ's FCPA enforcement program. He argued that the answer is not to manufacture cases, or to prosecute individuals based on legal interpretations contrary to the intent of Congress in enacting the FCPA while at the same time failing to prosecute individuals in connection with the most egregious cases of corporate bribery.

Michael Volkov

Attorney Michael Volkov advocated the adoption of a limited amnesty program for corporate self-compliance with the FCPA. Volkov's proposal consists of the following elements:

1. Participating company agrees to conduct a full and complete review of the company's FPCA compliance program for the five previous years.
2. This internal review is to be conducted, jointly, by a major accounting firm or specialized forensic accounting firm and a law firm.
3. The company agrees to disclose the results of the legal-accounting audit to the DOJ, Securities and Exchange Commission (SEC), its investors and the public.
4. If the company discovers any FPCA violations in the audit, the Company agrees to take all steps to eliminate the violation(s) and implement appropriate controls to prevent further violations.
5. The company would subject itself to an annual

review for five years to ensure that FCPA compliance was maintained.

6. The company would retain a person similar to an independent FCPA compliance monitor who would annually certify to the DOJ and SEC that the company was in FCPA compliance.
7. In exchange for this, both the DOJ and SEC would agree not to initiate any enforcement actions against a company during this period except in the situation where a FCPA violation was found and it "rose to ***flagrant*** or ***egregious*** levels."

Andrew Wiessman

Attorney Andrew Wiessmann testified about 2 of his 5 proposed amendments to the FCPA (the full five proposed amendments are set out in Whitepaper entitled "*Restoring Balance-Proposed Amendments to the Foreign Corrupt Practices Act*"). They were (1) to create a compliance defense available to a company if it has an adequate compliance program, similar to the "*adequate procedures*" defense available under the UK Bribery Act; and (2) to limit the legal doctrine of *respondeat superior* liability where a company can demonstrate that it took specific steps to prevent the offending employee's actions.

Under this proposal, Wiessmann believes that companies will increase their compliance with the FCPA because they will now have a greater incentive to do so. He envisions a defense similar to the "*adequate procedures*" defense, noted in the UK Bribery Act, where companies will be protected if a rogue employee engages in corruption and bribery despite a company's diligence in pursuing a FCPA compliance program; and lastly "it will give corporations some measure of protection from aggressive or misinformed prosecutors, who can exploit the power imbalance inherent in the current FCPA statute—which permits indictment of a corporation even for the acts of a single, low-level rogue employee—to force corporations into deferred prosecution agreements."

Most interestingly, the hearing began with the Subcommittee Chairperson, Senator Arlen Specter, questioning the DOJ's policy of obtaining large fines from corporations, rather than prosecuting individuals, to deter violation of the law. He specifically cited the example of the enforcement action against Siemens Corp., which resulted in a fine of $1.6 billion, yet had no individual prosecutions. He also pointed to the examples of BAE which paid a fine of $400 million and the Daimler Corporation which paid a fine of $185 million and subsequently there have been no individuals prosecuted from either of these corporations. Senator Specter posed the question to the DOJ representative at the hearing, Greg Andres, as to whether the imposition of fines simply was viewed by companies as a cost of doing business. Senator Specter's statements were clearly in opposite to the testimony of the three witnesses who seemed to be calling for more defenses, greater clarity and an amnesty program.

James McGrath

Another practitioner, Cleveland attorney James McGrath, also weighed in with a proposal for an amendment to respond to what he called "seismic shift in the government's perception of its role" regarding internal company FCPA investigations. Responding to Lanny Breuer's advise that when a possible FCPA violation has been discovered, a corporation should "seek the government's input on the front end of its internal investigation", McGrath proposed an amendment to the FCPA that would expressly prohibit requiring a company to immediately involve the DOJ at the outset of the internal investigation process as mandatory for receiving cooperation credit under the US Sentencing Guidelines. He argued that for those companies that do invite the government in as investigatory partners from the beginning, there should be some transactional or use immunity -- or at least some limitation on penalties and sanctions -- for other wrongs uncovered during the course of the FCPA investigation in recognition of their good-faith efforts to cooperate with the government. Such legislation amending the FCPA would protect the balance of interests in corporate criminal and civil prosecutions already struck by the US Sentencing Guidelines.

II. Bribery Act

Q: Why is a UK law on our Top FPCA issues for 2010?

A: Because it is a ***game changer.***

Passed in April 2010 and set to become effective on April 1, 2011, the UK Bribery Act represents what former DOJ prosecutor and now private practitioner Mark Mendelsohn is quoted in the Wall Street Journal to have said "is the FCPA on steroids." In the December 28, 2010 article entitled "*U.K. Law On Bribes Has Firms In a Sweat*", reporter Dionne Searcey indicated that the Bribery Act replaces several old British statutes and codifies in one location, that country's laws against bribery in the commercial context. Although Searcey called the law's scope "murky" the UK Ministry of Justice has released preliminary guidance on a key component of the Bribery Act; what may constitute an adequate compliance program.

This is important because there is one affirmative defense listed in the Bribery Act and it is listed as the "*adequate procedures*" defense. The Explanatory Notes to the Bribery Act indicate that this narrow defense would allow a corporation to put forward credible evidence that it had adequate procedures in place to prevent persons associated from committing bribery offences. The legislation required the UK Ministry of Justice to publish guidance on procedures that relevant commercial organizations can put in place to prevent bribery by persons associated with their entity. The Ministry of Justice published its guidance in September and took comments from interested parties. The final guidance is scheduled to be made available in early 2011. This guidance may well set the new worldwide *best practices* for a corporate anti-bribery and anti-corruption program.

- In addition to providing substantive guidance on what may constitute the basis for the only affirmative defense under the Bribery Act, there are several substantive differences between the FPCA and the UK Bribery Act which all companies should understand. The Bribery Act:
    - ◊ has no exception for facilitation payments.
    - ◊ creates strict liability of corporate offense for the failure of a corporate official to prevent bribery.
    - ◊ specifically prohibits the bribery or attempted bribery of private citizens, not just governmental officials.
    - ◊ not only bans the actual or attempted bribery of private citizens and public officials but all the receipt of such bribes.
    - ◊ has criminal penalties of up to 10 years per offense not 5 years as under the FCPA.

The Bribery Act is a significant departure for the UK in the area of foreign anti-corruption. It cannot be emphasized too strongly that the Bribery Act is significantly stronger than the FCPA. The Bribery Act provides for two general types of offence: bribing and being bribed, and for two further specific offences of bribing a foreign public official and corporate failure to prevent bribery. All the offences apply to behavior taking place either inside the UK, or outside it provided the person has a "close connection" with the UK. A person has a "close connection" if they were, at the relevant time, among other things, a British citizen, an individual ordinarily resident in the UK, or a body incorporated under the law of any part of the UK. Many internationally focused US companies have offices in the UK or employ UK citizens in their worldwide operations. This legislation could open them to prosecution in the UK under a law similar to, but stronger than, the relevant US legislation.

One positive development from the Bribery Act is that it does away with any legal question of "who is a foreign governmental official" which is often a question under the FCPA. The DOJ uses other legislation, such as the Travel Act, which can be used to ban commercial bribery generally, to back corrupt actions made to a foreign person who is not a governmental official, into an FCPA violation. The Bribery Act simply bans all commercial bribery. All US companies with UK subsidiaries or UK citizens as employees, needs to understand how this law will impact their operations and should integrate the Bribery Act's *adequate procedures* into their overall compliance and ethics policies sooner rather than later.

III. FCPA Based Litigation

1. Your Dog Bit Me – Alba

As reported by the FCPA Blog, the Aluminum Bahrain BSC., known as Alba, is majority-owned by the government of Bahrain. It has filed two lawsuits against its own suppliers, alleging corruption and fraud against it by the suppliers. In the first suit, Alba sued Alcoa Inc., its long-time raw materials supplier, for corruption and fraud. The suit, in Federal court in Pittsburg, alleged that over a 15-year period Alba was overcharged $2 billion for materials. This money, according to the suit, was initially paid to overseas accounts controlled by Alcoa's agent, London-based Victor Dahdaleh, and some was then used to bribe Alba's executives in return for supply contracts.

In the second suit, Alba claimed that the Japanese trading company Sojitz Corp. and its US subsidiary paid $14.8 million in bribes to two of Alba's employees in exchange for access to metals at below-market prices. Alba sought money damages in both suits. An interesting development in both suits has been that the DOJ intervened saying discovery could interfere with the governments' own investigation into potential criminal wrongdoing, including possible violations of the FCPA.

2. How Fast Can You Get to the Courthouse – SciClone

SciClone is the most recent example of a fast growing trend that occurs when some type of FCPA investigation is announced, of law firms pouncing with lawsuits claiming securities violations before the investigations are concluded. As reported by the FCPA Professor, on August 9th, SciClone announced that it had been contacted by the SEC and was advised that the SEC had initiated a formal, non-public investigation. In connection with this investigation, the SEC had issued a subpoena to SciClone requesting a variety of documents and other information. The subpoena requested documents relating to a range of matters including interactions with regulators and government-owned entities in China; activities relating to sales in China and documents relating to certain company financial and other disclosures. On August 6th, 2010, the Company had received a letter from the DOJ indicating that it was investigating FCPA issues in the pharmaceutical industry generally, and had received information about the Company's practices suggesting possible violations. Within the week, its stock dropped over 31%. Within one week, 5 law firms announced that they were investigating the company for potential securities laws investigation and within 2 weeks, seven different law firms had filed class actions suits against the company for securities violations.

3. Don't Do as I Do, Do as I Say - Noisy Exits

This past year brought a growing trend for terminated employees to file suit claiming that they were fired for either (1) reporting allegations of conduct violative of the FCPA or (2) refusing to engage in conduct which would violate the FCPA.

A recent example of the former was reported by the FCPA Professor in a post entitled "*Yet Another Noisy Exit*". In this matter, the former Director and Controller of Mexico-based Sempra Global, Rodolfo Michelon, was terminated by the company in March 2010. He later alleged that he discovered conduct by the company in Mexico which violated the FCPA; he subsequently reported this to the company and was fired for his efforts. In a California state court suit, he claimed that "The termination of the Controller employment was not only in retaliation for Michelon's complaints, but it was also meant to keep Michelon from reporting the frauds and bribes to governmental, law enforcement officials." The Company vehemently denied these allegations, responding, as reported in the San Diego Tribune, that Michelon was a "disgruntled ex-employee attempting to cash in by making 'outlandishly false claims and misrepresentations' after being let go in a routine reorganization." The company also noted that it had investigated the allegations and found them to be "without merit."

An example of the later claim was brought by Steven Jacobs, the former President of Macau Operations for Las Vegas Sands Corp., until his termination in July 2010. In a suit against the Las Vegas Sands Corp., alleging breach of contract and tort-based causes of action, Jacobs alleged, among other things, that he was ordered, but refused, to use improper leverage and undue influence on certain Chinese governmental officials so as to obtain favorable treatment for his employer in China. Additionally, he alleged that he was required "to use the legal services of a Macau attorney [...][an individual media is reporting as a member of a Chinese local government executive council] despite concerns that [the individual's] retention posed serious risks under the criminal provisions of the United States code commonly known as the Foreign Corrupt Practices Act ('FCPA')." As noted by the FCPA Professor the company has stated, "While Las Vegas Sands normally does not comment on legal matters, we categorically deny these baseless and inflammatory allegations."

4. Law Students Enter the FCPA Debate

Two law students blogged about law review articles, scheduled to be published in 2010, which greatly enhanced the FCPA world in the past year.

UCLA student Kyle Sheahen explored the issue of affirmative defenses under the FCPA in an article entitled "*I'm Not Going to Disneyland: Illusory Affirmative Defenses Under the Foreign Corrupt Practices Act*". In his paper, he sets forth his proposition that FCPA enforcement actions provide "uneven indicators or what conduct the government considers covered by the defense. Consequently, in the absence of authoritative judicial interpretation or clear regulatory guidance, corporate managers are required to make educated guesses as to whether contemplated payments will qualify as "bona fide promotional expenses."

Bruce Hinchey discussed his upcoming publication, "*Punishing the Penitent: Disproportionate Fines in Recent FCPA Enforcements and Suggested Improvements*," which analyzes the differences between bribes paid and penalties levied against companies that do and do not self-disclose under the FCPA. Using a regression analysis, Hinchey concluded that companies which did voluntarily self-disclose paid higher fines than companies which did not. He concluded his post by noting that this evidence was contrary to the conventional wisdom that a company receives a benefit from self-disclosure and such evidence would "raise questions about whether current FCPA enforcement is fundamentally fair".

While we disagreed with some of the conclusions of both Sheahan and Hinchey, we found their contributions enhanced the FCPA discussions for the compliance practitioner. To have law students penning authoritative law review articles signals an upcoming group of lawyers who will bring a passion to the FCPA debates in the future. We wish them both well as they enter the FCPA fray as attorneys.

So we leave this most eventful FCPA year of 2010 and move into 2011. With all we have learned in the past year, the only thing we can say with certainty is "*more will be revealed*".

We appreciate the support of all readers, contributors, commentators and critics of our blog. A very Happy and Safe New Year's to all.

Suspension of FCPA is NOT the Solution

Posted March 30, 2010

Should enforcement of the Foreign Corrupt Practices Act (FCPA) be suspended for those US companies now working in Haiti? This topic has been in discussion for a few weeks. It began with a statement by Wall Street Journal editorial board member Mary Anastasia O'Grady in a piece entitled "*Democrats and Haiti Telecom*". Ms. O'Grady cited "an American entrepreneur" for the quote "We did not bother with Haiti as the Foreign Corrupt Practices Act precludes legitimate U.S. entities from entering the Haitian market. Haiti is pure pay to play".

This *"pay to play"* statement led George Mason University Professor Tyler Cowen, writing in the Marginal Revolution Blog, to write "one of the best ways to help Haiti" is to "pass a law stating that the Foreign Corrupt Practices Act does not apply to dealings in Haiti. As it stands right now, U.S. businesses are unwilling to take on this legal risk and the result is similar to an embargo. You can't do business in Haiti without paying bribes". Professor Cowen's statement led Eric Lipman, writing in the Legal Blog Watch, to follow this up with "[i]t should not be necessary to suspend enforcement of an anti-corruption law to enable U.S. companies to participate, but, realistically speaking, is it justified in this case to look the other way for a time?".

Responding to the suggestion that FCPA enforcement

should be suspended in Haiti, the FCPA Professor articulated three reasons the law should not be suspended in Haiti. First the FCPA applies only to foreign governmental officials so not all business dealings in Haiti are covered by the FCPA. Second, empirical evidence suggests that foreign investment will be high in countries as Haiti if their markets are lucrative, but Haiti's is not. Third, is Haiti's 2009 ranking in Transparency International's Corruption Perceptions Index which demonstrates that it is a country where corruption is rampant.

As the lead editorial in its Sunday, March 28 edition, the New York Times urged that Haiti "will need to sweep out the old, bad ways of doing things, not only those of the infamously corrupt and hapless government, but also of aid and development agencies, whose nurturing of Haiti has been a manifest failure for more than half a century". The piece suggested the following ideas to further this goal: Transparency, Accountability and Effectiveness; Haitian Involvement, Self-Sufficiency; Tapping the Diaspora and De-centralization as some of the keys for a successful rebuilding of Haiti. These ideas applied to groups both inside the country and out. But it is clear that the Times did not suggest that cow-towing to a "*pay to play state*" by suspending the enforcement of the FCPA was a way to move forward.

APPENDIX I

TEXT OF THE FOREIGN CORRUPT PRACTICES ACT

Text of The Foreign Corrupt Practices Act

UNITED STATES CODE
TITLE 15. COMMERCE AND TRADE
CHAPTER 2B – SECURITIES EXCHANGES
§ 78m. Periodical and other reports

(a) Reports by issuer of security; contents

Every issuer of a security registered pursuant to section 781 of this title shall file with the Commission, in accordance with such rules and regulations as the Commission may prescribe as necessary or appropriate for the proper protection of investors and to insure fair dealing in the security—

(1) such information and documents (and such copies thereof) as the Commission shall require to keep reasonably current the information and documents required to be included in or filed with an application or registration statement filed pursuant to section 781 of this title, except that the Commission may not require the filing of any material contract wholly executed before July 1, 1962.

(2) such annual reports (and such copies thereof), certified if required by the rules and Regulations of the Commission by independent public accountants, and such quarterly reports (and such copies thereof), as the Commission may prescribe. Every issuer of a security Registered on a national securities exchange shall also

file a duplicate original of such information, Documents, and reports with the exchange.

(b) Form of report; books, records, and internal accounting; directives (2) Every issuer which has a class of securities registered pursuant to section 78l of this title and every issuer which is required to file reports pursuant to section 78o(d) of this title shall — (A) make and keep books, records, and accounts, which, in reasonable detail, accurately and fairly reflect the transactions and dispositions of the assets of the issuer; and (B) devise and maintain a system of internal accounting controls sufficient to provide reasonable assurances that— (i) transactions are executed in accordance with management's general or specific authorization; (ii) transactions are recorded as necessary (I) to permit preparation of financial statements in conformity with generally accepted accounting principles or any other criteria applicable to such statements, and (II) to maintain accountability for assets; (iii) access to assets is permitted only in accordance with management's general or specific authorization; and (iv) the recorded accountability for assets is compared with the existing assets at reasonable intervals and appropriate action is taken with respect to any differences.

(3) (A) With respect to matters concerning the national security of the United States, no duty or
liability under paragraph (2) of this subsection shall be imposed upon any person acting in cooperation with the head of any Federal department or agency responsible for such matters if such act in cooperation with such head of a department or agency was done upon the specific, written directive of the head of such department or agency pursuant to Presidential authority to issue such directives. Each directive issued under this paragraph

shall set forth the specific facts and circumstances with respect to which the provisions of this paragraph are to be invoked. Each such directive shall, unless renewed in writing, expire one year after the date of issuance.

(B) Each head of a Federal department or agency of the United States who issues such a directive pursuant to this paragraph shall maintain a complete file of all such directives and shall, on October 1 of each year, transmit a summary of matters covered by such directives in force at any time during the previous year to the Permanent Select Committee on Intelligence of the House of Representatives and the Select Committee on Intelligence of the Senate.

(4) No criminal liability shall be imposed for failing to comply with the requirements of Paragraph (2) of this subsection except as provided in paragraph (5) of this subsection.

(5) No person shall knowingly circumvent or knowingly fail to implement a system of internal accounting controls or knowingly falsify any book, record, or account described in paragraph (2).

(6) Where an issuer which has a class of securities registered pursuant to section 78l of this title or an issuer which is required to file reports pursuant to section 78o(d) of this title holds 50 per centum or less of the voting power with respect to a domestic or foreign firm, the provisions of paragraph (2) require only that the issuer proceed in good faith to use its influence, to the extent reasonable under the issuer's circumstances, to cause such domestic or foreign firm to devise and maintain a system of internal accounting controls consistent with paragraph (2). Such circumstances include the relative degree of the issuer's ownership of the domestic or foreign firm and the laws

and practices governing the business operations of the country in which such firm is located. An issuer which demonstrates good faith efforts to use such influence shall be conclusively presumed to have complied with the requirements of paragraph (2).

(7) For the purpose of paragraph (2) of this subsection, the terms "reasonable assurances" and "reasonable detail" mean such level of detail and degree of assurance as would satisfy prudent officials in the conduct of their own affairs.§ 78dd-1. Prohibited foreign trade practices by issuers

(a) Prohibition

It shall be unlawful for any issuer which has a class of securities registered pursuant to section 78l of this title or which is required to file reports under section 78o(d) of this title, or for any officer, director, employee, or agent of such issuer or any stockholder thereof acting on behalf of such issuer, to make use of the mails or any means or instrumentality of interstate commerce corruptly in furtherance of an offer, payment, promise to pay, or authorization of the payment of any money, or offer, gift, promise to give, or authorization of the giving of anything of value to— (1) any foreign official for purposes of— (A) (i) influencing any act or decision of such foreign official in his official capacity, (ii) inducing such foreign official to do or omit to do any act in violation of the lawful duty of such official, or (iii) securing any improper advantage; or (B) inducing such foreign official to use his influence with a foreign government or instrumentality thereof to affect or influence any act or decision of such government or instrumentality, in order to assist such issuer in obtaining or retaining business for or with, or directing business to, any person;

(2) any foreign political party or official thereof or any candidate for foreign political office for purposes of— (A) (i) influencing any act or decision of such party, official, or candidate in its or his official capacity, (ii) inducing such party, official, or candidate to do or omit to do an act in violation of the lawful duty of such party, official, or candidate, or (iii) securing any improper advantage; or (B) inducing such party, official, or candidate to use its or his influence with a foreign government or instrumentality thereof to affect or influence any act or decision of such government or instrumentality in order to assist such issuer in obtaining or retaining business for or with, or directing business to, any person; or

(3) any person, while knowing that all or a portion of such money or thing of value will be offered, given, or promised, directly or indirectly, to any foreign official, to any foreign political party or official thereof, or to any candidate for foreign political office, for purposes of—

(A) (i) influencing any act or decision of such foreign official, political party, party official, or candidate in his or its official capacity, (ii) inducing such foreign official, political party, party official, or candidate to do or omit to do any act in violation of the lawful duty of such foreign official, political party, party official, or candidate, or (iii) securing any improper advantage; or (B) inducing such foreign official, political party, party official, or candidate to use his or its influence with a foreign government or instrumentality thereof to affect or influence any act or decision of such government or instrumentality, in order to assist such issuer in obtaining or retaining business for or with, or directing business to, any person.

(b) Exception for routine governmental action Subsections (a) and (g) of this section shall not apply to any facilitating or expediting payment to a foreign official, political party, or party official the purpose of which is to expedite or to secure the performance of a routine governmental action by a foreign official, political party, or party official.

(c) Affirmative defenses

It shall be an affirmative defense to actions under subsection (a) or (g) of this section that— (1) the payment, gift, offer, or promise of anything of value that was made, was lawful under the written laws and regulations of the foreign official's, political party's, party official's, or candidate's country; or (2) the payment, gift, offer, or promise of anything of value that was made, was a reasonable and bona fide expenditure, such as travel and lodging expenses, incurred by or on behalf of a foreign official, party, party official, or candidate and was directly related to— (A) the promotion, demonstration, or explanation of products or services; or (B) the Execution or performance of a contract with a foreign government or agency thereof.

(d) Guidelines by Attorney General

Not later than one year after August 23, 1988, the Attorney General, after consultation with the Commission, the Secretary of Commerce, the United States Trade Representative, the Secretary of State, and the Secretary of the Treasury, and after obtaining the views of all interested persons through public notice and comment procedures, shall determine to what extent compliance with this section would be enhanced and the business community would be assisted by further clarification of the preceding provisions of this section and may, based on such determination and to the extent necessary and appropriate, issue— (1) guidelines describing specific

types of conduct, associated with common types of export sales arrangements and business contracts, which for purposes of the Department of Justice's present enforcement policy, the Attorney General determines would be in conformance with the preceding provisions of this section; and (2) general precautionary procedures which issuers may use on a voluntary basis to conform their conduct to the Department of Justice's present enforcement policy regarding the preceding
provisions of this section. The Attorney General shall issue the guidelines and procedures referred to in the preceding sentence in accordance with the provisions of subchapter II of chapter 5 of Title 5 and those guidelines and procedures shall be subject to the provisions of chapter 7 of that title.

(e) Opinions of Attorney General

(1) The Attorney General, after consultation with appropriate departments and agencies of the United States and after obtaining the views of all interested persons through public notice and comment procedures, shall establish a procedure to provide responses to specific inquiries by issuers concerning conformance of their conduct with the Department of Justice's present enforcement policy regarding the preceding provisions of this section. The Attorney General shall, within 30 days after receiving such a request, issue an opinion in response to that request. The opinion shall state whether or not certain specified prospective conduct would, for purposes of the Department of Justice's present enforcement policy, violate the preceding provisions of this section. Additional requests for opinions may be filed with the Attorney General regarding other specified prospective conduct that is beyond the scope

of conduct specified in previous requests. In any action brought under the applicable provisions of this section, there shall be a rebuttable presumption that conduct, which is specified in a request by an issuer and for which the Attorney General has issued an opinion that such conduct is in conformity with the Department of Justice's present enforcement policy, is in compliance with the preceding provisions of this section. Such a presumption may be rebutted by a preponderance of the evidence. In considering the presumption for purposes of this paragraph, a court shall weigh all relevant factors, including but not limited to whether the information submitted to the Attorney General was accurate and complete and whether it was within the scope of the conduct specified in any request received by the Attorney General. The Attorney General shall establish the procedure required by this paragraph in accordance with the provisions of subchapter II of chapter 5 of Title 5 and that procedure shall be subject to the provisions of chapter 7 of that title. (2) Any document or other material which is provided to, received by, or prepared in the Department of Justice or any other department or agency of the United States in connection with a request by an issuer under the procedure established under paragraph (1), shall be exempt from disclosure under section 552 of Title 5 and shall not, except with the consent of the issuer, be made publicly available, regardless of whether the Attorney General responds to such a request or the issuer withdraws such request before receiving a response. (3) Any issuer who has made a request to the Attorney General under paragraph (1) may withdraw such request prior to the time the Attorney General issues an opinion in response to such request. Any request so withdrawn shall have no force or effect. (4) The Attorney General shall, to the maximum extent practicable, provide timely guidance concerning the Department of Justice's present enforcement policy with respect to the preceding provisions of this section to potential exporters and small businesses that are unable to obtain specialized counsel on issues pertaining to such provisions. Such guidance shall be limited to responses to requests under paragraph (1) concerning conformity of specified prospective conduct with the Department of Justice's present enforcement policy regarding the preceding provisions of this section and general explanations of compliance responsibilities and of potential liabilities under the preceding provisions of this section.

(f) Definitions

For purposes of this section: (1) (A) The term "foreign official" means any officer or employee of a foreign government or any department, agency, or instrumentality thereof, or of a public international organization, or any person acting in an official capacity for or on behalf of any such government or department, agency, or instrumentality, or for or on behalf of any such public international organization. (B) For purposRs of subparagraph (A), the term "public international organization" means—(i) an organization that is designated by Executive Order pursuant to section 1 of the International Organizations Immunities Act (22 U.S.C. § 288); or (ii) any other international organization that is designated by the President by Executive Order for the purposes of this section, effective as of the date of publication of such order in the Federal Register.

(2) (A) A person's state of mind is "knowing" with respect to conduct, a circumstance, or a result if—(i)

such person is aware that such person is engaging in such conduct, that such circumstance exists, or that such result is substantially certain to occur; or (ii) such person has a firm belief that such circumstance exists or that such result is substantially certain to occur. (B) When knowledge of the existence of a particular circumstance is required for an offense, such knowledge is established if a person is aware of a high probability of the existence of such circumstance, unless the person actually believes that such circumstance does not exist.(3) (A) The term routine governmental action" means only an action which is ordinarily and commonly performed by a foreign official in—(i) obtaining permits, licenses, or other official documents to qualify a person to do business in a foreign country; (ii) processing governmental papers, such as visas and work orders; (iii) providing police protection, mail pick-up and delivery, or scheduling inspections associated with contract performance or inspections related to transit of goods across country; (iv) providing phone service, power and water supply, loading and unloading cargo, or protecting perishable products or commodities from deterioration; or (v) actions of a similar nature.

(B) The term "routine governmental action" does not include any decision by a foreign official whether, or on what terms, to award new business to or to continue business with a particular party, or any action taken by a foreign official involved in the decision-making process to encourage a decision to award new business to or continue business with a particular party.

(g) Alternative Jurisdiction

(1) It shall also be unlawful for any issuer organized under the laws of the United States, or a State, territory,

possession, or commonwealth of the United States or a political subdivision thereof and which has a class of securities registered pursuant to section 12 of this title or which is required to file reports under section 15(d) of this title, or for any United States person that is an officer, director, employee, or agent of such issuer or a stockholder thereof acting on behalf of such issuer, to corruptly do any act outside the United States in furtherance of an offer, payment, promise to pay, or authorization of the payment of any money, or offer, gift, promise to give, or authorization of the giving of anything of value to any of the persons or entities set forth in paragraphs (1), (2), and (3) of this subsection (a) of this section for the purposes set forth therein, irrespective of whether such issuer or such officer, director, employee, agent, or stockholder makes use of the mails or any means or instrumentality of interstate commerce in furtherance of such offer, gift, payment, promise, or authorization.

(2) As used in this subsection, the term "United States person means a national of the United States (as defined in section 101 of the Immigration and Nationality Act (8 U.S.C. § 1101)) or any corporation, partnership, association, joint-stock company, business trust, unincorporated organization, or sole proprietorship organized under the laws of the United States or any State, territory, possession, or commonwealth of the United States, or any political subdivision thereof. § 78dd-2. Prohibited foreign trade practices by domestic concerns

(a) Prohibition

It shall be unlawful for any domestic concern, other than an issuer which is subject to section 78dd-1 of this title, or for any officer, director, employee, or agent of such domestic concern or any stockholder thereof acting on behalf of such domestic concern, to make use of the mails or any means or instrumentality of interstate commerce corruptly in furtherance of an offer, payment, promise to pay, or authorization of the payment of any money, or offer, gift, promise to give, or authorization of the giving of anything of value to— (1) any foreign official for purposes of— (A) (i) influencing any act or decision of such foreign official in his official capacity, (ii) inducing such foreign official to do or omit to do any act in violation of the lawful duty of such official, or (iii) securing any improper advantage; or (B) inducing such foreign official to use his influence with a foreign government or instrumentality thereof to affect or influence any act or decision of such government or instrumentality, in order to assist such domestic concern in obtaining or retaining business for or with, or directing business to, any person; (2) any foreign political party or official thereof or any candidate for foreign political office for purposes of— (A) (i) influencing any act or decision of such party, official, or candidate in its or his official capacity, (ii) inducing such party, official, or candidate to do or omit to do an act in violation of the lawful duty of such party, official, or candidate, or (iii) securing any improper advantage; or (B) inducing such party, official, or candidate to use its or his influence with a foreign government or instrumentality thereof to affect or influence any act or decision of such government or instrumentality, in order to assist such domestic concern in obtaining or retaining business for or with, or directing business to, any person; (3) any person, while knowing that all or a portion of such money or thing of value will be offered, given, or promised, directly or indirectly, to any foreign official,

to any foreign political party or official thereof, or to any candidate for foreign political office, for purposes of—
(A) (i) influencing any act or decision of such foreign official, political party, party official, or candidate in his or its official capacity, (ii) inducing such foreign official, political party, party official, or candidate to do or omit to do any act in violation of the lawful duty of such foreign official, political party, party official, or candidate, or (iii) securing any improper advantage; or
(B) inducing such foreign official, political party, party official, or candidate to use his or its influence with a foreign government or instrumentality thereof to affect or influence any act or decision of such government or instrumentality, in order to assist such domestic concern in obtaining or retaining business for or with, or directing business to, any person.
(b) Exception for routine governmental action
Subsections (a) and (i) of this section shall not apply to any facilitating or expediting payment to a foreign official, political party, or party official the purpose of which is to expedite or to secure the performance of a routine governmental action by a foreign official, political party, or party official.
(c) Affirmative defenses
It shall be an affirmative defense to actions under subsection (a) or (i) of this section that— (1) the payment, gift, offer, or promise of anything of value that was made, was lawful under the written laws and regulations of the foreign official's, political party's, party official's, or candidate's country; or (2) the payment, gift, offer, or promise of anything of value that was made, was a reasonable and bona fide expenditure, such as travel and lodging expenses, incurred by or on behalf of a foreign

official, party, party official, or candidate and was directly related to— (A) the promotion, demonstration, or explanation of products or services; or (B) the execution or performance of a contract with a foreign government or agency thereof.

(d) Injunctive relief

(1) When it appears to the Attorney General that any domestic concern to which this section applies, or officer, director, employee, agent, or stockholder thereof, is engaged, or about to engage, in any act or practice constituting a violation of subsection (a) or (i) of this section, the Attorney General may, in his discretion, bring a civil action in an appropriate district court of the United States to enjoin such act or practice, and upon a proper showing, a permanent injunction or a temporary restraining order shall be granted without bond.

(2) For the purpose of any civil investigation which, in the opinion of the Attorney General, is necessary and proper to enforce this section, the Attorney General or his designee are empowered to administer oaths and affirmations, subpoena witnesses, take evidence, and require the production of any books, papers, or other documents which the Attorney General deems relevant or material to such investigation. The attendance of witnesses and the production of documentary evidence may be required from any place in the United States, or any territory, possession, or commonwealth of the United States, at any designated place of hearing.

(3) In case of contumacy by, or refusal to obey a subpoena issued to, any person, the Attorney General may invoke the aid of any court of the United States within the jurisdiction of which such investigation or proceeding is carried on, or where such person resides or carries on

business, in requiring the attendance and testimony of witnesses and the production of books, papers, or other documents. Any such court may issue an order requiring such person to appear before the Attorney General or his designee, there to produce records, if so ordered, or to give testimony touching the matter under investigation. Any failure to obey such order of the court may be punished by such court as a contempt thereof.

All process in any such case may be served in the judicial district in which such person resides or may be found. The Attorney General may make such rules relating to civil investigations as may be necessary or appropriate to implement the provisions of this subsection.

(e) Guidelines by Attorney General

Not later than 6 months after August 23, 1988, the Attorney General, after consultation with the Securities and Exchange Commission, the Secretary of Commerce, the United States Trade Representative, the Secretary of State, and the Secretary of the Treasury, and after obtaining the views of all interested persons through public notice and comment procedures, shall determine to what extent compliance with this section would be enhanced and the business community would be assisted by further clarification of the preceding provisions of this section and may, based on such determination and to the extent necessary and appropriate, issue— (1) guidelines describing specific types of conduct, associated with common types of export sales arrangements and business contracts, which for purposes of the Department of Justice's present enforcement policy, the Attorney General determines would be in conformance with the preceding provisions of this section; and (2) general precautionary procedures which domestic concerns may use on a voluntary basis to conform their conduct to the Department of Justice's present enforcement policy regarding the preceding provisions of this section. The Attorney General shall issue the guidelines and procedures referred to in the preceding sentence in accordance with the provisions of subchapter II of chapter 5 of Title 5 and those guidelines and procedures shall be subject to the provisions of chapter 7 of that title.

(f) Opinions of Attorney General

(1) The Attorney General, after consultation with appropriate departments and agencies of the United States and after obtaining the views of all interested persons through public notice and comment procedures, shall establish a procedure to provide responses to specific inquiries by domestic concerns concerning conformance of their conduct with the Department of Justice's present enforcement policy regarding the preceding provisions of this section. The Attorney General shall, within 30 days after receiving such a request, issue an opinion in response to that request. The opinion shall state whether or not certain specified prospective conduct would, for purposes of the Department of Justice's present enforcement policy, violate the preceding provisions of this section. Additional requests for opinions may be filed with the Attorney General regarding other specified prospective conduct that is beyond the scope of conduct specified in previous requests. In any action brought under the applicable provisions of this section, there shall be a rebuttable presumption that conduct, which is specified in a request by a domestic concern and for which the Attorney General has issued an opinion that such conduct is in conformity with the Department of Justice's present enforcement policy, is in compliance

with the preceding provisions of this section. Such a presumption may be rebutted by a preponderance of the evidence. In considering the presumption for purposes of this paragraph, a court shall weigh all relevant factors, including but not limited to whether the information submitted to the Attorney General was accurate and complete and whether it was within the scope of the conduct specified in any request received by the Attorney General. The Attorney General shall establish the procedure required by this paragraph in accordance with the provisions of subchapter II of chapter 5 of Title 5 and that procedure shall be subject to the provisions of chapter 7 of that title.

(2) Any document or other material which is provided to, received by, or prepared in the Department of Justice or any other department or agency of the United States in connection with a request by a domestic concern under the procedure established under paragraph (1), shall be exempt from disclosure under section 552 of Title 5 and shall not, except with the consent of the domestic concern, be made publicly available, regardless of whether the Attorney General response to such a request or the domestic concern withdraws such request before receiving a
response.

(3) Any domestic concern who has made a request to the Attorney General under paragraph (1) may withdraw such request prior to the time the Attorney General issues an opinion in response to such request. Any request so withdrawn shall have no force or effect.

(4) The Attorney General shall, to the maximum extent practicable, provide timely guidance concerning the Department of Justice's present enforcement policy

with respect to the preceding provisions of this section to potential exporters and small businesses that are unable to obtain specialized counsel on issues pertaining to such provisions. Such guidance shall be limited to responses to requests under paragraph (1) concerning conformity of specified prospective conduct with the Department of Justice's present enforcement policy regarding the preceding provisions of this section and general explanations of compliance responsibilities and of potential liabilities under the preceding provisions of this section.

(g) Penalties

(1) (A) Any domestic concern that is not a natural person and that violates subsection (a) or (i) of this section shall be fined not more than $2,000,000.

(B) Any domestic concern that is not a natural person and that violates subsection (a) or (i) of this section shall be subject to a civil penalty of not more than $10,000 imposed in an action brought by the Attorney General.

(2) (A) Any natural person that is an officer, director, employee, or agent of a domestic concern, or stockholder acting on behalf of such domestic concern, who willfully violates subsection (a) or (i) of this section shall be fined not more than $100,000 or imprisoned not more than 5 years, or both.

(B) Any natural person that is an officer, director, employee, or agent of a domestic concern, or stockholder acting on behalf of such domestic concern, who violates subsection (a) (i) of this section shall be subject to a civil penalty of not more than $10,000 imposed in an action brought by the Attorney General.

(3) Whenever a fine is imposed under paragraph (2) upon any officer, director, employee, agent, or stockholder of a

domestic concern, such fine may not be paid, directly or indirectly, by such domestic concern.

(h) Definitions

For purposes of this section:

(1) The term "domestic concern" means—

(A) any individual who is a citizen, national, or resident of the United States; and

(B) any corporation, partnership, association, joint-stock company, business trust, unincorporated organization, or sole proprietorship which has its principal place of business in the United States, or which is organized under the laws of a State of the United States or a territory, possession, or commonwealth of the United States.

(2) (A) The term "foreign official" means any officer or employee of a foreign government or any department, agency, or instrumentality thereof, or of a public international organization, or any person acting in an official capacity for or on behalf of any such government or department, agency, or instrumentality, or for or on behalf of any such public international organization.

(B) For purposes of subparagraph (A), the term "public international organization" means —

(i) an organization that has been designated by Executive order pursuant to Section 1 of the International Organizations Immunities Act (22 U.S.C. § 288); or

(ii) any other international organization that is designated by the President by Executive order for the purposes of this section, effective as of the date of publication of such order in the Federal Register.

(3) (A) A person's state of mind is "knowing" with respect to conduct, a circumstance, or a result if—(i) such person is aware that such person is engaging in such conduct, that such circumstance exists, or that such result

is substantially certain to occur; or
(ii) such person has a firm belief that such circumstance exists or that such result is substantially certain to occur.
(B) When knowledge of the existence of a particular circumstance is required for an offense, such knowledge is established if a person is aware of a high probability of the existence of such circumstance, unless the person actually believes that such circumstance does not exist.
(4) (A) The term "routine governmental action" means only an action which is ordinarily and
commonly performed by a foreign official in— (i) obtaining permits, licenses, or other official documents to qualify a person to do business in a foreign country;
(ii) processing governmental papers, such as visas and work orders;
(iii) providing police protection, mail pick-up and delivery, or scheduling inspections associated with contract performance or inspections related to transit of goods across country;
(iv) providing phone service, power and water supply, loading and unloading cargo, or protecting perishable products or commodities from deterioration; or
(v) actions of a similar nature.
(B) The term "routine governmental action" does not include any decision by a foreign official whether, or on what terms, to award new business to or to continue business with a particular party, or any action taken by a foreign official involved in the decision-making process to encourage a decision to award new business to or continue business with a particular party.
(5) The term "interstate commerce" means trade, commerce, transportation, or communication
among the several States, or between any foreign country

and any State or between any State and any place or ship outside thereof, and such term includes the intrastate use of— (A) a telephone or other interstate means of communication, or

(B) any other interstate instrumentality.

(i) Alternative Jurisdiction

(1) It shall also be unlawful for any United States person to corruptly do any act outside the United States in furtherance of an offer, payment, promise to pay, or authorization of the payment of any money, or offer, gift, promise to give, or authorization of the giving of anything of value to any of the persons or entities set forth in paragraphs (1), (2), and (3) of subsection (a), for the purposes set forth therein, irrespective of whether such United States person makes use of the mails or any means or instrumentality of interstate commerce in furtherance of such offer, gift, payment, promise, or authorization.

(2) As used in this subsection, a "United States person means a national of the United States (as defined in section 101 of the Immigration and Nationality Act (8 U.S.C. § 1101)) or any corporation, partnership, association, joint-stock company, business trust, unincorporated organization, or sole proprietorship organized under the laws of the United States or any State, territory, possession, or commonwealth of the United States, or any political subdivision thereof. §78dd-3. Prohibited foreign trade practices by persons other than issuers or domestic concerns

(a) Prohibition

It shall be unlawful for any person other than an issuer that is subject to section 30A of the Securities Exchange Act of 1934 or a domestic concern, as defined in section 104 of this Act, or for any officer, director, employee, or agent of such person or any stockholder thereof acting on behalf of such person, while in the territory of the United States, corruptly to make use of the mails or any means or instrumentality of interstate commerce or to do any other act in furtherance of an offer, payment, promise to pay, or authorization of the payment of any money, or offer, gift, promise to give, or authorization of the giving of anything of value to—

(1) any foreign official for purposes of—

(A) (i) influencing any act or decision of such foreign official in his official capacity, (ii) inducing such foreign official to do or omit to do any act in violation of the lawful duty of such

official, or (iii) securing any improper advantage; or (B) inducing such foreign official to use his influence with a foreign government or instrumentality thereof to affect or influence any act or decision of such government or instrumentality, in order to assist such person in obtaining or retaining business for or with, or directing business to, any person;

(2) any foreign political party or official thereof or any candidate for foreign political office for

purposes of— (A) (i) influencing any act or decision of such party, official, or candidate in its or his official capacity, (ii) inducing such party, official, or candidate to do or omit to do an act in violation of the lawful duty of such party, official, or candidate, or (iii) securing any improper advantage; or

(B) inducing such party, official, or candidate to use its or his influence with a foreign government or instrumentality thereof to affect or influence any act or decision of such government or instrumentality, in order to assist such person in obtaining or retaining business for or with, or

directing business to, any person; or
(3) any person, while knowing that all or a portion of such money or thing of value will be offered, given, or promised, directly or indirectly, to any foreign official, to any foreign political party or official thereof, or to any candidate for foreign political office, for purposes of—
(A) (i) influencing any act or decision of such foreign official, political party, party official, or candidate in his or its official capacity, (ii) inducing such foreign official, political party, party official, or candidate to do or omit to do any act in violation of the lawful duty of such foreign official, political party, party official, or candidate, or (iii) securing any improper
advantage; or
(B) inducing such foreign official, political party, party official, or candidate to use his or its influence with a foreign government or instrumentality thereof to affect or influence any act or decision of such government or instrumentality, in order to assist such person in obtaining or retaining business for or with, or directing business to, any person.
(b) Exception for routine governmental action
Subsection (a) of this section shall not apply to any facilitating or expediting payment to a foreign official, political party, or party official the purpose of which is to expedite or to secure the performance of a routine governmental action by a foreign official, political party, or party official.
(c) Affirmative defenses
It shall be an affirmative defense to actions under subsection (a) of this section that— (1) the payment, gift, offer, or promise of anything of value that was made, was lawful under the written laws and regulations of

the foreign official's, political party's, party official's, or candidate's country; or

(2) the payment, gift, offer, or promise of anything of value that was made, was a reasonable and bona fide expenditure, such as travel and lodging expenses, incurred by or on behalf of a foreign official, party, party official, or candidate and was directly related to— (A) the promotion, demonstration, or explanation of products or services; or (B) the execution or performance of a contract with a foreign government or agency thereof.

(d) Injunctive relief

(1) When it appears to the Attorney General that any person to which this section applies, or officer, director, employee, agent, or stockholder thereof, is engaged, or about to engage, in any act or practice constituting a violation of subsection (a) of this section, the Attorney General may, in his discretion, bring a civil action in an appropriate district court of the United States to enjoin such act or practice, and upon a proper showing, a permanent injunction or a temporary restraining order shall be granted without bond.

(2) For the purpose of any civil investigation which, in the opinion of the Attorney General, is necessary and proper to enforce this section, the Attorney General or his designee are empowered to administer oaths and affirmations, subpoena witnesses, take evidence, and require the production of any books, papers, or other documents which the Attorney General deems relevant or material to such investigation. The attendance of witnesses and the production of documentary evidence may be required from any place in the United States, or any territory, possession, or commonwealth of the United States, at any designated place of hearing.

(3) In case of contumacy by, or refusal to obey a subpoena issued to, any person, the Attorney General may invoke the aid of any court of the United States within the jurisdiction of which such investigation or proceeding is carried on, or where such person resides or carries on business, in requiring the attendance and testimony of witnesses and the production of books, papers, or other documents. Any such court may issue an order requiring such person to appear before the Attorney General or his designee, there to produce records, if so ordered, or to give testimony touching the matter under investigation. Any failure to obey such order of the court may be punished by such court as a contempt thereof.

(4) All process in any such case may be served in the judicial district in which such person resides or may be found. The Attorney General may make such rules relating to civil investigations as may be necessary or appropriate to implement the provisions of this subsection.

(e) Penalties

(1) (A) Any juridical person that violates subsection (a) of this section shall be fined not more than $2,000,000.

(B) Any juridical person that violates subsection (a) of this section shall be subject to a civil penalty of not more than $10,000 imposed in an action brought by the Attorney General.

(2) (A) Any natural person who willfully violates subsection (a) of this section shall be fined not more than $100,000 or imprisoned not more than 5 years, or both.

(B) Any natural person who violates subsection (a) of this section shall be subject to a civil penalty of not more than $10,000 imposed in an action brought by the Attorney General.

(3) Whenever a fine is imposed under paragraph (2) upon

any officer, director, employee, agent, or stockholder of a person, such fine may not be paid, directly or indirectly, by such person.

(f) Definitions

For purposes of this section:

(1) The term "person, when referring to an offender, means any natural person other than a national of the United States (as defined in 8 U.S.C. § 1101) or any corporation, partnership, association, joint-stock company, business trust, unincorporated organization, or sole proprietorship organized under the law of a foreign nation or a political subdivision thereof.

(2) (A) The term "foreign official" means any officer or employee of a foreign government or any department, agency, or instrumentality thereof, or of a public international organization, or any person acting in an official capacity for or on behalf of any such government or department, agency, or instrumentality, or for or on behalf of any such public international organization.

(B) For purposes of subparagraph (A), the term "public international organization" means —(i) an organization that has been designated by Executive Order pursuant to Section 1 of the International Organizations Immunities Act (22 U.S.C. § 288); or

(ii) any other international organization that is designated by the President by Executive order for the purposes of this section, effective as of the date of publication of such order in the Federal Register.

(3) (A) A person's state of mind is "knowing" with respect to conduct, a circumstance, or a
result if—

(i) such person is aware that such person is engaging in such conduct, that such circumstance exists, or that such result is substantially certain to occur; or (ii) such person has a firm belief that such circumstance exists or that such result is substantially certain to occur.

(B) When knowledge of the existence of a particular circumstance is required for an offense, such knowledge is established if a person is aware of a high probability of the existence of such circumstance, unless the person actually believes that such circumstance does not exist.

(4) (A) The term "routine governmental action" means only an action which is ordinarily and

commonly performed by a foreign official in—(i) obtaining permits, licenses, or other official documents to qualify a person to do business in a foreign country;

(ii) processing governmental papers, such as visas and work orders;

(iii) providing police protection, mail pick-up and delivery, or scheduling inspections associated with contract performance or inspections related to transit of goods across country;

(iv) providing phone service, power and water supply, loading and unloading cargo, or protecting perishable products or commodities from deterioration; or (v) actions of a similar nature.

(B) The term "routine governmental action" does not include any decision by a foreign official whether, or on what terms, to award new business to or to continue business with a particular party, or any action taken by a foreign official involved in the decision-making process to encourage a decision to award new business to or continue business with a particular party.

(5) The term "interstate commerce" means trade, commerce, transportation, or communication among the several States, or between any foreign country and any

State or between any State and any place or ship outside thereof, and such term includes the intrastate use of—(A) a telephone or other interstate means of communication, or

(B) any other interstate instrumentality.

§ 78ff. Penalties

(a) Willful violations; false and misleading statements

Any person who willfully violates any provision of this chapter (other than section 78dd-1 of this title), or any rule or regulation thereunder the violation of which is made unlawful or the observance of which is required under the terms of this chapter, or any person who willfully and knowingly makes, or causes to be made, any statement in any application, report, or document required to be filed under this chapter or any rule or regulation thereunder or any undertaking contained in a registration statement as provided in subsection (d) of section 78o of this title, or by any self-regulatory organization in connection with an application for membership or participation therein or to become associated with a member thereof, which statement was false or misleading with respect to any material fact, shall upon conviction be fined not more than $5,000,000, or imprisoned not more than 20 years, or both, except that when such person is a person other than a natural person, a fine not exceeding $25,000,000 may be imposed; but no person shall be subject to imprisonment under this section for the violation of any rule or regulation if he proves that he had no knowledge of such rule or regulation.

(b) Failure to file information, documents, or reports

Any issuer which fails to file information, documents, or reports required to be filed under subsection (d) of section

78o of this title or any rule or regulation thereunder shall forfeit to the United States the sum of $100 for each and every day such failure to file shall continue. Such forfeiture, which shall be in lieu of any criminal penalty for such failure to file which might be deemed to arise under subsection (a) of this section, shall be payable into the Treasury of the United States and shall be recoverable in a civil suit in the name of the United States.

(c) Violations by issuers, officers, directors, stockholders, employees, or agents of

Issuers (1) (A) Any issuer that violates subsection (a) or (g) of section 78dd-1 of this title shall be fined not more than $2,000,000.

(B) Any issuer that violates subsection (a) or (g) of section 78dd-1 of this title shall be subject to a civil penalty of not more than $10,000 imposed in an action brought by the Commission.

(2) (A) Any officer, director, employee, or agent of an issuer, or stockholder acting on behalf of such issuer, who willfully violates subsection (a) or (g) of section 78dd-1 of this title shall be fined not more than $100,000, or imprisoned not more than 5 years, or both.

(B) Any officer, director, employee, or agent of an issuer, or stockholder acting on behalf of such issuer, who violates subsection (a) or (g) of section 78dd-1 of this title shall be subject to a civil penalty of not more than $10,000 imposed in an action brought by the Commission.

(3) Whenever a fine is imposed under paragraph (2) upon any officer, director, employee, agent, or stockholder of an issuer, such fine may not be paid, directly or indirectly, by such issue.

APPENDIX II

A LAYMAN'S GUIDE TO THE FOREIGN CORRUPT PRACTICES ACT (FCPA)

A LAYMAN'S GUIDE TO THE FCPA

INTRODUCTION

The 1988 Trade Act directed the Attorney General to provide guidance concerning the Department of Justice's enforcement policy with respect to the Foreign Corrupt Practices Act of 1977 ("FCPA"), 15 U.S.C. §§ 78dd-1, et seq., to potential exporters and small businesses that are unable to obtain specialized counsel on issues related to the FCPA. The guidance is limited to responses to requests under the Department of Justice's Foreign Corrupt Practices Act Opinion Procedure (described below at p. 10) and to general explanations of compliance responsibilities and potential liabilities under the FCPA. This brochure constitutes the Department of Justice's general explanation of the FCPA. U.S. firms seeking to do business in foreign markets must be familiar with the FCPA. In general, the FCPA prohibits corrupt payments to foreign officials for the purpose of obtaining or keeping business. In addition, other statutes such as the mail and wire fraud statutes, 18 U.S.C. § 1341, 1343, and the Travel Act, 18 U.S.C. § 1952, which provides for federal prosecution of violations of state commercial bribery statutes, may also apply to such conduct.

The Department of Justice is the chief enforcement agency, with a coordinate role played by the Securities and Exchange Commission (SEC). The Office of General Counsel of the Department of Commerce also answers general questions from U.S. exporters concerning the FCPA's basic requirements and constraints. This brochure is intended to provide a general description of the FCPA and is not intended to substitute for the advice of private counsel on specific issues related to the FCPA. Moreover, material in this brochure is not intended to set forth the present enforcement intentions of the Department of Justice or the SEC with respect to particular fact situations.

BACKGROUND

As a result of SEC investigations in the mid-1970's, over 400 U.S. companies admitted making questionable or illegal payments in excess of $300 million to foreign government officials, politicians, and political parties. The abuses ran the gamut from bribery of high foreign officials to secure some type of favorable action by a foreign government to so-called facilitating payments that allegedly were made to ensure that government functionaries discharged certain ministerial or clerical duties. Congress enacted the FCPA to bring a halt to the bribery of foreign officials and to restore public confidence in the integrity of the American business system.

The FCPA was intended to have and has had an enormous impact on the way American firms do business. Several firms that paid bribes to foreign officials have been the subject of criminal and civil enforcement actions, resulting in large fines and suspension and debarment from federal procurement contracting, and their employees and officers have gone to jail. To avoid such consequences, many firms have implemented detailed compliance programs intended to prevent and to detect any improper payments by employees and agents.

Following the passage of the FCPA, the Congress became concerned that American companies were operating at a disadvantage compared to foreign companies who routinely paid bribes and, in some countries, were permitted to deduct the cost of such bribes as business expenses on their taxes. Accordingly, in 1988, the Congress directed the Executive Branch to commence negotiations in the Organization of Economic Cooperation and Development (OECD) to obtain the agreement of the United States' major trading partners to enact legislation similar to the FCPA. In 1997, almost ten years later, the United States and thirty-three other countries signed the OECD Convention on Combating Bribery of Foreign Public Officials in International Business Transactions. The United States ratified this Convention and enacted implementing legislation in 1998. See Convention and Commentaries on the DOJ web site.

The anti-bribery provisions of the FCPA make it unlawful for a U.S. person, and certain foreign issuers of securities, to make a corrupt payment to a foreign official for the purpose of obtaining or retaining business for or with, or directing business to, any person. Since 1998, they also apply to foreign firms and persons who take any act in furtherance of such a corrupt payment while in the United States.

The FCPA also requires companies whose securities are listed in the United States to meet its accounting provisions. See 15 U.S.C. § 78m. These accounting provisions, which were designed to operate in tandem with the anti-bribery provisions of the FCPA, require corporations covered by the provisions to make and keep books and records that accurately and fairly reflect the transactions of the corporation and to devise and maintain an adequate system of internal accounting controls. This brochure discusses only the anti-bribery provisions.

ENFORCEMENT

The Department of Justice is responsible for all criminal enforcement and for civil enforcement of the anti-bribery provisions with respect to domestic concerns and foreign companies and nationals. The SEC is responsible for civil enforcement of the anti-bribery provisions with respect to issuers.

ANTIBRIBERY PROVISIONS

BASIC PROHIBITION

The FCPA makes it unlawful to bribe foreign government officials to obtain or retain business. With respect to the basic prohibition, there are five elements which must be met to constitute a violation of the Act:

A. Who -- The FCPA potentially applies to any individual, firm, officer, director, employee, or agent of a firm and any stockholder acting on behalf of a firm. Individuals and firms may also be penalized if they order, authorize, or assist someone else to violate the anti-bribery provisions or if they conspire to violate those provisions.

Under the FCPA, U.S. jurisdiction over corrupt payments to foreign officials depends upon whether the violator is an "issuer," a "domestic concern," or a foreign national or business. An "issuer" is a corporation that has issued securities that have been registered in the United States or who is required to file periodic reports with the SEC. A "domestic concern" is any individual who is a citizen, national, or resident of the United States, or any corporation, partnership, association, joint-stock company, business trust, unincorporated organization, or sole proprietorship which has its principal place of business in the United States, or which is organized under the laws of a State of the United States, or a territory, possession, or commonwealth of the United States.

Issuers and domestic concerns may be held liable under the FCPA under either territorial or nationality jurisdiction principles. For acts taken within the territory of the United States, issuers and domestic concerns are liable if they take an act in furtherance of a corrupt payment to a foreign official using the U.S. mails or other means or instrumentalities of interstate commerce. Such means or instrumentalities include telephone calls, facsimile transmissions, wire transfers, and interstate or international travel. In addition, issuers and domestic concerns may be held liable for any act in furtherance of a corrupt payment taken outside the United States. Thus, a U.S. company or national may be held liable for a corrupt payment authorized by employees or agents operating entirely outside the United States, using money from foreign bank accounts, and without any involvement by personnel located within the United States.

Prior to 1998, foreign companies, with the exception of those who qualified as "issuers," and foreign nationals were not covered by the FCPA. The 1998 amendments expanded the FCPA to assert territorial jurisdiction over foreign companies and nationals. A foreign company or person is now subject to the FCPA if it causes, directly or through agents, an act in furtherance of the corrupt payment to take place within the territory of the United States. There is, however, no requirement that such act make use of the U.S. mails or other means or instrumentalities of interstate commerce.

Finally, U.S. parent corporations may be held liable for the acts of foreign subsidiaries where they authorized, directed, or controlled the activity in question, as can U.S. citizens or residents, themselves "domestic concerns," who were employed by or acting on behalf of such foreign-incorporated subsidiaries.

B. Corrupt intent -- The person making or authorizing the payment must have a corrupt intent, and the payment must be intended to induce the recipient to misuse his official position to direct business wrongfully to the payer or to any other person. You should note that the FCPA does not require that a corrupt act succeed in its purpose. The offer or promise of a corrupt payment can constitute a violation of the statute. The FCPA prohibits any corrupt payment intended to influence any act or decision of a foreign official in his or her official capacity, to induce the official to do or omit to do any act in violation of his or her lawful duty, to obtain any improper advantage, or to induce a foreign official to use his or her influence improperly to affect or influence any act or decision.

C. Payment -- The FCPA prohibits paying, offering, promising to pay (or authorizing to pay or offer) money or anything of value.

D. Recipient -- The prohibition extends only to corrupt payments to a foreign official, a foreign political party or party official, or any candidate for foreign political office. A "foreign official" means any officer or employee of a foreign government, a public international organization, or any department or agency thereof, or any person acting in an official capacity.

You should consider utilizing the Department of Justice's Foreign Corrupt Practices Act Opinion Procedure for particular questions as to the definition of a "foreign official," such as whether a member of a royal family, a member of a legislative body, or an official of a state-owned business enterprise would be considered a "foreign official."

The FCPA applies to payments to any public official, regardless of rank or position. The FCPA focuses on the purpose of the payment instead of the particular duties of the official receiving the payment, offer, or promise of payment, and there are exceptions to the anti-bribery provision for "facilitating payments for routine governmental action" (see below).

E. Business Purpose Test -- The FCPA prohibits payments made in order to assist the firm in obtaining or retaining business for or with, or directing business to, any person. The Department of Justice interprets "obtaining or retaining business" broadly, such that the term encompasses more than the mere award or renewal of a contract. It should be noted that the business to be obtained or retained does not need to be with a foreign government or foreign government instrumentality.

THIRD PARTY PAYMENTS

The FCPA prohibits corrupt payments through intermediaries. It is unlawful to make a payment to a third party, while knowing that all or a portion of the payment will go directly or indirectly to a foreign official. The term "knowing" includes conscious disregard and deliberate ignorance. The elements of an offense are essentially the same as described above, except that in this case the "recipient" is the intermediary who is making the payment to the requisite "foreign official."

Intermediaries may include joint venture partners or agents. To avoid being held liable for corrupt third party payments, U.S. companies are encouraged to exercise due diligence and to take all necessary precautions to ensure that they have formed a business relationship with reputable and qualified partners and representatives. Such due diligence may include investigating potential foreign representatives and joint venture partners to determine if they are in fact qualified for the position, whether they have personal or professional ties to the government, the number and reputation of their clientele, and their reputation with the U.S. Embassy or Consulate and with local bankers, clients, and other business associates. In addition, in negotiating a business relationship, the U.S. firm should be aware of so-called "red flags," i.e., unusual payment patterns or financial arrangements, a history of corruption in the country, a refusal by the foreign joint venture partner or representative to provide a certification that it will not take any action in furtherance of an unlawful offer, promise, or payment to a foreign public official and not take any act that would cause the U.S. firm to be in violation of the FCPA, unusually high commissions, lack of transparency in expenses and accounting records, apparent lack of qualifications or resources on the part of the joint venture partner or representative to perform the services offered, and whether the joint venture partner or representative has been recommended by an official of the potential governmental customer.

You should seek the advice of counsel and consider utilizing the Department of Justice's Foreign Corrupt Practices Act Opinion Procedure for particular questions relating to third party payments.

PERMISSIBLE PAYMENTS AND AFFIRMATIVE DEFENSES

The FCPA contains an explicit exception to the bribery prohibition for "facilitating payments" for "routine governmental action" and provides affirmative defenses which can be used to defend against alleged violations of the FCPA.

FACILITATING PAYMENTS FOR ROUTINE GOVERNMENTAL ACTIONS

There is an exception to the anti-bribery prohibition for payments to facilitate or expedite performance of a "routine governmental action." The statute lists the following examples: obtaining permits, licenses, or other official documents; processing governmental papers, such as visas and work orders; providing police protection, mail pick-up and delivery; providing phone service, power and water supply, loading and unloading cargo, or protecting perishable products; and scheduling inspections associated with contract performance or transit of goods across country.

Actions "similar" to these are also covered by this exception. If you have a question about whether a payment falls within the exception, you should consult with counsel. You should also consider whether to utilize the Justice Department's Foreign Corrupt Practices Opinion Procedure, described below on p. 10.

"Routine governmental action" does not include any decision by a foreign official to award new business or to continue business with a particular party.

AFFIRMATIVE DEFENSES

A person charged with a violation of the FCPA's anti-bribery provisions may assert as a defense that the payment was lawful under the written laws of the foreign country or that the money was spent as part of demonstrating a product or performing a contractual obligation. Whether a payment was lawful under the written laws of the foreign country may be difficult to determine. You should consider seeking the advice of counsel or utilizing the Department of Justice's Foreign Corrupt Practices Act Opinion Procedure when faced with an issue of the legality of such a payment.

Moreover, because these defenses are "affirmative defenses," the defendant is required to show in the first instance that the payment met these requirements. The prosecution does not bear the burden of demonstrating in the first instance that the payments did not constitute this type of payment.

SANCTIONS AGAINST BRIBERY

CRIMINAL

The following criminal penalties may be imposed for violations of the FCPA's anti-bribery provisions: corporations and other business entities are subject to a fine of up to $2,000,000; officers, directors, stockholders, employees, and agents are subject to a fine of up to $100,000 and imprisonment for up to five years. Moreover, under the Alternative Fines Act, these fines may be actually quite higher -- the actual fine may be up to twice the benefit that the defendant sought to obtain by making the corrupt payment. You should also be aware that fines imposed on individuals may not be paid by their employer or principal.

CIVIL

The Attorney General or the SEC, as appropriate, may bring a civil action for a fine of up to $10,000 against any firm as well as any officer, director, employee, or agent of a firm, or stockholder acting on behalf of the firm, who violates the anti-bribery provisions. In addition, in an SEC enforcement action, the court may impose an additional fine not to exceed the greater of (i) the gross amount of the pecuniary gain to the defendant as a result of the violation, or (ii) a specified dollar limitation. The specified dollar limitations are based on the egregiousness of the violation, ranging from $5,000 to $100,000 for a natural person and $50,000 to $500,000 for any other person.

The Attorney General or the SEC, as appropriate, may also bring a civil action to enjoin any act or practice of a firm whenever it appears that the firm (or an officer, director, employee, agent, or stockholder acting on behalf of the firm) is in violation (or about to be) of the antibribery provisions.

OTHER GOVERNMENTAL ACTION

Under guidelines issued by the Office of Management and Budget, a person or firm found in violation of the FCPA may be barred from doing business with the Federal government. Indictment alone can lead to suspension of the right to do business with the government. The President has directed that no executive agency shall allow any party to participate in any procurement or non-procurement activity if any agency has debarred, suspended, or otherwise excluded that party from participation in a procurement or non-procurement activity. In addition, a person or firm found guilty of violating the FCPA may be ruled ineligible to receive export licenses; the SEC may suspend or bar persons from the securities business and impose civil penalties on persons in the securities business for violations of the FCPA; the Commodity Futures Trading Commission and the Overseas Private Investment Corporation both provide for possible suspension or debarment from agency programs for violation of the FCPA; and a payment made to a foreign government official that is unlawful under the FCPA cannot be deducted under the tax laws as a business expense.

PRIVATE CAUSE OF ACTION

Conduct that violates the anti-bribery provisions of the FCPA may also give rise to a private cause of action for treble damages under the Racketeer Influenced and Corrupt Organizations Act (RICO), or to actions under other federal or state laws. For example, an action might be brought under RICO by a competitor who alleges that the bribery led to the defendant winning a foreign contract.

GUIDANCE FROM THE GOVERNMENT

The Department of Justice has established a Foreign Corrupt Practices Act Opinion Procedure by which any U.S. company or national may request a statement of the Justice Department's present enforcement intentions under the anti-bribery provisions of the FCPA regarding any proposed business conduct. The details of the opinion procedure may be found at 28 CFR Part 80. Under this procedure, the Attorney General will issue an opinion in response to a specific inquiry from a person or firm within thirty days of the request. (The thirty-day period does not begin to run until the Department of Justice has received all the information it requires to issue the opinion.) Conduct for which the Department of Justice has issued an opinion stating that the conduct conforms with current enforcement policy will be entitled to a presumption, in any subsequent enforcement action, of conformity with the FCPA. Copies of releases issued regarding previous opinions are available on the Department of Justice's FCPA web site.

For further information from the Department of Justice about the FCPA and the Foreign Corrupt Practices Act Opinion Procedure, contact Charles Duross, Deputy Chief, Fraud Section, at (202) 353-7691; or Nathaniel Edmonds, Assistant Chief, Fraud Section, at (202) 307-0629; or William Stuckwisch, Assistant Chief, Fraud Section, at (202) 353-2393.

Although the Department of Commerce has no enforcement role with respect to the FCPA, it supplies general guidance to U.S. exporters who have questions about the FCPA and about international developments concerning the FCPA. For further information from the Department Commerce about the FCPA contact Eleanor Roberts Lewis, Chief Counsel for International Commerce, or Arthur Aronoff, Senior Counsel, Office of the Chief Counsel for International Commerce, U.S. Department of Commerce, Room 5882, 14th Street and Constitution Avenue, N.W., Washington, D.C. 20230, (202) 482-0937

United States Department of Justice
Fraud Section, Criminal Division
10th & Constitution Ave. NW (Bond 4th fl.)
Washington, D.C. 20530
Phone: (202) 514-7023
Fax: (202) 514-7021
Internet: http://www.justice.gov/criminal/fraud/fcpa
Email: FCPA.fraud@usdoj.gov
United States Department of Commerce
Office of the Chief Counsel for International Commerce
14th Street and Constitution Avenue, NW
Room 5882
Washington, D.C. 20230
Phone: (202) 482-0937
Fax: (202) 482-4076

Internet: http://www.ita.doc.gov/legal

Index

A

B

C

D

L

M

N

O

P

R

S

T

U

V

W

Z